T0347651

CHARLES DICKENS

My Reading

ANNETTE FEDERICO

CHARLES
DICKENS

But for You, Dear Stranger

OXFORD
UNIVERSITY PRESS

OXFORD
UNIVERSITY PRESS

Great Clarendon Street, Oxford, OX2 6DP,
United Kingdom

Oxford University Press is a department of the University of Oxford.
It furthers the University's objective of excellence in research, scholarship,
and education by publishing worldwide. Oxford is a registered trade mark of
Oxford University Press in the UK and in certain other countries

© Annette Federico 2022

First Edition published in 2022
Impression: 1

Published in the United States of America by Oxford University Press
198 Madison Avenue, New York, NY 10016, United States of America

British Library Cataloguing in Publication Data
Data available

Library of Congress Control Number: 2022935479

ISBN 978-0-19-284734-8

DOI: 10.1093/oso/9780192847348.001.0001

Printed and bound in the UK by
Clays Ltd, Elcograf S.p.A.

Links to third party websites are provided by Oxford in good faith and
for information only. Oxford disclaims any responsibility for the materials
contained in any third party website referenced in this work.

For Chuck,
and in memory of my parents

SERIES INTRODUCTION

This series is built on a simple presupposition: that it helps to have a book recommended and discussed by someone who cares for it. Books are not purely self-sufficient: they need people and they need to get to what is personal within them.

The people we have been seeking as contributors to *My Reading* are readers who are also writers: novelists and poets; literary critics, outside as well as inside universities, but also thinkers from other disciplines—philosophy, psychology, science, theology, and sociology—beside the literary; and, not least of all, intense readers whose first profession is not writing itself but, for example, medicine, or law, or a non-verbal form of art. Of all of them we have asked: what books or authors feel as though they are deeply *yours*, influencing or challenging your life and work, most deserving of rescue and attention, or demanding of feeling and use?

What is it like to love this book? What is it like to have a thought or idea or doubt or memory, not cold and in abstract, but live in the very act of reading? What is it like to feel, long after, that this writer is a vital part of your life? We ask our authors to respond to such bold questions by writing not conventionally but personally—whatever "personal" might mean, whatever form or style it might take, for them as individuals. This does not mean overt confession at the expense of a chosen book or author; but nor should our writers be afraid of making autobiographical connections. What was wanted was whatever made for their own hardest thinking in careful relation to quoted sources and specifics. The work was to go on in the taut and resonant space between these readers and their chosen books. And the interest within that area begins precisely when it is no longer clear how much is coming from the text, and how much is coming from its readers—where that distinction is no longer easily tenable because neither is sacrificed to the other. That would show what reading meant at its most serious and how it might have relation to an individual life.

Out of what we hope will be an ongoing variety of books and readers, *My Reading* offers personal models of what it is like to care about particular authors, to recreate through specific examples imaginative versions of what those authors and works represent, and to show their effect upon a reader's own thinking and development.

ANNE CHENG

PHILIP DAVIS

JACQUELINE NORTON

MARINA WARNER

MICHAEL WOOD

PREFACE

When I started to think about a book for the *My Reading* series, my mind went to a few different authors, some I knew well, others I wanted to know better. I tried to listen to my feelings as I hunted for a writer who meant something personal to me, who seemed necessary just at this moment in the world's timeline, and in my sixtieth decade of living. Then one day, looking out the kitchen window as I sipped my morning coffee, it struck me with quite sudden certainty that the author I had to write about was Charles Dickens. But how surprising. I never thought of myself as a Dickens expert. I haven't even read everything Dickens wrote. Outside of *The Uncommercial Traveller*, I have barely touched his journalism, and know only a handful of his shorter pieces of fiction. Some of the early novels—*The Pickwick Papers*, *The Old Curiosity Shop*, *Barnaby Rudge*, *Martin Chuzzlewit*, *Nicholas Nickleby*—I have read only once or twice, a long time ago. Yet somehow, I knew Dickens was the one. I knew he was the writer who seems to have informed my life most meaningfully, and that I wanted to revisit his writing for this series. But I still didn't quite know why.

Dickens was an astute observer of his society, of course. But Dickens the social critic, the progressive and reformer, is not the writer who speaks most confidentially to me. To say that a Dickens novel is an attack on industrial capitalism or that it is about a particular side of human character—selfishness in *Martin Chuzzlewit*, pride in *Dombey and Son*, snobbery in *Great Expectations*—does not match the nuance of Dickens's observations about the way modern people live their lives. Dickens writes with gusto and sociability, and his dramatic imagination is astounding. No writer in the world uses his physical senses the way Dickens does. Yet he is also a quietly susceptive writer, with a great responsive delicacy. He is psychological and intuitive, attuned to all the shades of human emotion. As I reread the novels for this book, I tried to pay attention to what magnetized me or drew me in, to what struck me as newly relevant to my life. What is the story *emotionally* about? This became the important question for me—the question that opened the door to my own memories, my own stories.

My choice of Dickens for this series is personal in another way. Dickens is a rebuke to arrogance and creeping negativity. He writes about good people because he believed there were good people in the world, as I do. He writes hopefully, not because he is a blindly optimistic Victorian, but because he has a grudge against despair. Dickens sees vividly the misery and suffering in his society, and as he aged his perspective darkened. But he knows it just doesn't help anyone to be like Mrs. Gummidge (before her conversion). You have to take a position about your life, and about the future. Pessimism and bitterness are not viable attitudes for Dickens. Sadness and regret, yes, for these things are unavoidable in human life. But never cynicism.

The three novels I reflect on were written between 1837 and 1859. The first numbers of *Oliver Twist* appeared in *Bentley's Miscellany* in February 1837, four months before Victoria became queen, and less than a year after Dickens's marriage to Catherine Hogarth. Dickens was 25, and already on his way to becoming famous. *David Copperfield* was serialized in *Household Words* ten years later, in 1849–50. It stands exactly in the middle of Dickens's career, when he was at the height of his professional success (and the father of seven children). The last number of *Little Dorrit* appeared in June of 1857, when Dickens was 45. Four months later he saw an 18-year-old actress named Ellen Ternan perform in a play in Doncaster; in June 1859, he and his wife Catherine separated. *A Tale of Two Cities*, the subject of my final short chapter, was serialized in Dickens's new magazine, *All the Year Round*, between May and November of that year.

A chronology of my life as a reader of Dickens is embedded in this book, running parallel to my life as a daughter, a spouse, a teacher, a scholar. I have tried not to let that last role loom too largely, though. In a letter from January 1859, Dickens outlined his desired legacy: "I hope I have done my part to make the rising generation 'more childish,' in rendering them a little more imaginative, a little more gentle, and a little less conceited and hard, than they would have been without me. I desire to do nothing better." To grow more childish is a reverse education, a pilgrimage away from mere intellectual knowingness toward some other kind of knowledge. It is to see the world more believingly and imaginatively, with a little less guile, perhaps, and less reliance on other people's opinions. This book also attempts that backwards journey.

CONTENTS

LIST OF FIGURES

1

WHERE IS LOVE?

My father died in a nursing home on March 26, 2017 at the age of 95. Two and a half years later, one month and two days before her 94th birthday, my mother died in a hospital. Before the landslide of illnesses that jolted her from hospital to nursing home to rehab to hospital for over two months, she had been living quite contentedly by herself in the house my parents bought when I was born, in 1960. A modest house, as people like to say, on a modest suburban street on the east side of Cleveland, Ohio. A house that now needed to be cleaned and emptied of almost 60 years of accumulated junk in preparation for being sold.

My older brother, Tom, was my mother's executor, and because he lived in Cleveland, he was saddled with all of the organizing and the majority of the hauling. My older sister and I, the two out-of-towners, took turns coming home to do our share of the sorting, bagging, and boxing up of my parents' clothes, shoes, tools, recipe books, dishes, blankets, and many, many photos, papers, and tchotchkes—they didn't like to throw away anything that had links to our extended Italian-American family. My visit would also be my opportunity to take anything I wanted from the house, of sentimental or of practical value.

That fall was a difficult time for me. When my father died, I worried about how my mother would handle being without him after almost 70 years of marriage. When mom died, I felt I was dangling in mid-air, no one up there to extend a hand, no one below to catch me. Her death pushed me off balance. For many weeks that autumn, when I walked to and from campus to teach my classes, I had an eerie feeling that she was beside me or behind me, loving me, badgering me, laughing at me. Going about my regular routine with all of that confusion and depression inside me was like living two separate lives. A poem by Dorianne Laux, "For the Sake of Strangers," arrived in my inbox as my Poem of the Day during that time.

> No matter what the grief, its weight,
> we are obliged to carry it.
> We rise and gather momentum, the dull strength
> that pushes us through crowds.
> And then the young boy gives me directions
> so avidly. A woman holds the glass door open,
> waiting patiently for my empty body to pass through.
> All day it continues, each kindness
> reaching toward another—a stranger
> singing to no one as I pass on the path, trees
> offering their blossoms, a child
> who lifts his almond eyes and smiles.
>   Somehow they always find me, seem even
> to be waiting, determined to keep me
> from myself, from the thing that calls to me
> as it must have once called to them—
> this temptation to step off the edge
> and fall weightless, away from the world.[1]

"All day it continues," this unbearable gift of ordinary kindness. The autumn after Mom died, the turning leaves seemed especially bright, the skies all lucid blueness. Maybe the world—trees, people, children, dogs—always seems beautiful when you are dealing with grief. The bleakness that's inside jars against the sudden vividness of everything outside of you, until you're not sure what's real.

There is a short story by Chekhov called "Grief" (sometimes translated as "Misery" or "Heartbreak"). It is about a hired driver, Iona, whose son has recently died of a fever. He longs to tell someone what has happened to him. He is buried in grief, and has a pressing need to speak of it. But the gentlemen who hire his sledge are too drunk or preoccupied to listen to him. They shut him up with platitudes. At the end of the story, as night descends, Iona decides to look in on his mare, munching straw in the stables after a long evening's work. He starts to talk.

> "So it is, my little mare…Kuzma Ionitch is no more…Gave up the ghost…Just died for nothing…Now, suppose you had a little colt, and you're that little colt's own mother…And suddenly suppose that same little colt gives up the ghost…It's sad, isn't it?"
>
> The nag chews, listens, and breathes on her master's hands…Iona gets carried away and tells her everything…[2]

Chekhov's epigraph to the story is, "To whom shall I tell my grief?" I wonder if my parents felt like Iona when their eldest son, Joseph, died of cancer at the age of 49, and if they always wanted to talk more about him than they did? I loved my brother and I think about him often, but I will never comprehend what my parents went through. They clasped their grief closely between them for more than 20 years.

I thought of Chekhov's story that fall when I realized that, like Iona, and completely out of character for me, I was telling people I hardly knew about my mother's death—a colleague I ran into on my walk home, my teaching assistant, my dental hygienist, a little-known neighbor, the piano tuner, a gardener, my hair stylist. Virtual strangers. My inside world was on a sideway tilt, but they were operating in the normally proportioned world of everyday life. By telling people about my mother's death, I think I was trying to reach over to that world—to be on the other side of grieving.

Among the strangers I told about my loss was the friendly Uber driver who took me from my hotel to my parents' house on a Saturday morning in early November. We started with the usual chitchat, the awful weather that was here, the nice weather that was elsewhere. When he asked where I was from, I told him that Cleveland was my hometown but I had moved away for work decades ago, and now I was back because my mother had died. I had to clean things out of her house and set aside anything I wanted to keep. He said he was sorry, and that "she's better where she is." We speculated about whether or not the house would be haunted. I told him I hoped so.

My brother wanted me to start with the upstairs bedrooms. On a high shelf in the closet in the room I shared with my sister, I discovered boxes of stuff from my grade school and high school years—school reports, playbills, drama club photos, birthday cards, silly notes I'd passed in class. In one of the boxes, I found a typed rejection letter, dated September 9, 1970: "Dear Annette: Thank you for sending us your lovely illustrated Haiku poetry. Unfortunately, I must return it to you, because we no longer publish the magazine which printed children's work." The editor encouraged me to submit my poems to another magazine. She ended: "I hope that you will keep writing poetry—you seem to be sensitive and aware of the world around you, and able to express very well what you see and feel. Best of luck to you." Such generosity and kindness from an adult to a ten-year-old child! I don't remember anything about those illustrated haiku poems, but finding that letter was like discovering a lost part of myself.

I also unearthed two fat spiral notebooks absolutely crammed with poems and prose that needed to be preserved by teenage me as sources of wisdom. I was the thieving magpie of *Bartlett's Familiar Quotations*. Kahlil Gibran is ubiquitous. Aphorisms abound—Emerson and Thoreau, Stevenson, Goethe, John Henry Newman, Victor Hugo, Tagore, Blake, Montaigne, Whitman. I copied out poems by e.e. cummings, Shakespeare, Theodore Roethke, Robert Frost, Christina Rossetti, Anne Bradstreet, Edna St. Vincent Millay, John Clare, Longfellow, Wordsworth, Shelley, Keats, Ernest Dowson, and, bizarrely, Sir John Suckling. My father was a salesman for a printing company, and he was always bringing home scratchpads, stickers, posters, and booklets. I pasted images cut from my father's printing samples in creative word-and-image arrangements. I typed out Matthew Arnold's "The Buried Life" in its entirety and pasted it across two pages, like a sacred text. Not to discriminate against prose, I wrote out whole passages from Hardy's *Tess of the D'Urbervilles* and John Knowles's *A Separate Peace*, which we were reading in English class. I also wrote out the lyrics from Don McLean's bestselling album *American Pie*, and other sensitive-guy rock stars which I have long outgrown. But I have not outgrown Joni Mitchell, and she's in there too. I remember sitting on the carpeted floor in that very room listening to *Court and Spark* on Susan's portable record player, over and over. I liked "Big Yellow Taxi" because you wouldn't get the title unless you knew the lyrics. Once I asked Susan, who is seven years older, what her favorite song was. "'Trouble Child,'" she answered darkly.

I was astonished to find letters my family wrote to me when my grandmother and I flew to California, that far away and exotic land, to visit my great Aunt Sue and Uncle Nick, for my 12th birthday. My brothers and sister were obviously ordered to write to me, and their short, dutiful notes preserve the everydayness of our family routine. In Act III of Thornton Wilder's *Our Town*, after Emily dies in childbirth she longs to go back to the world just once more, on one ordinary day in her life—her 12th birthday, February 11, 1899. She watches her father shaking the snow off his feet, her mother preparing breakfast. "I can't look at everything hard enough," she says. The experience is so wrenching she breaks down sobbing and begs to be returned to the cemetery with the other ghosts. "I can't. I can't go on. It goes so fast. We don't have time to look at one another. I didn't realize. So all that was going on and we never noticed."[3] The letters my parents each wrote to me when I was away from home for the first time are heartrending in their unremarkableness. How happy they all seemed, how full their days were with just ordinary things, watching a baseball game, Tom's driving lessons, having a cook-out. I felt like a ghost, reading those letters alone in my old bedroom. All that was going on and I never noticed.

I was not looking forward to that weekend in my parents' cluttered house. My energy was depleted from an unusually busy semester, and I was still so sad. I anticipated an agonizing ritual. Yet being alone for many hours in that house, the house I have been going to and leaving with piercing ambivalence for my entire adult life, turned out to be a restoring and reconciling experience. My parents were both dead and things were going to change. But the dangling feeling was less frightening. I was learning about my parents. I found letters my mother had received from men she went to high school with who were in England during World War II. I found a beautiful album from their wedding shower in 1947, my sister's baby book from 1953, pictures I'd never seen of my gorgeous father when he was stationed in the Philippines. In their bedroom dresser I discovered a stash of what seemed to be every Mother's Day and Father's Day card we ever sent them. In my father's workbench I found all of my report cards and school projects, my stories and poems, my letters when I studied in Wales for my junior year abroad. All of our formal school photos were kept in a box, from every grade. I found a thick folder of my brother Joseph's school achievements, his diplomas, and all the postcards he sent to my parents when, as a college professor, he took students abroad to Germany and Austria. I discovered a photograph of him tucked into my mother's recliner.

My parents were open-hearted people. Joseph, who was eleven years older than I was, once said to me, "They're simple people." I didn't understand him—to me they seemed complicated, as all adults did. But maybe he meant they were from a simpler time. My grandparents on both sides were Italian immigrants. My mother's father was a jack-of-all trades with a temper, my father's father was a postal carrier and, very likely, an alcoholic. Mom and Dad grew up during the Depression. We heard stories about the ragman who would ride his pony through the neighborhood hawking his wares in broken English, and the waffle man and the knife man, singing street vendors, all from a vanished era. They both lived in Collinwood. It was a respectable neighborhood, but there were some tough people around, even Mafia types (my first cousin married a man who was best friends with the son of a well-known

Figure 1.1 Collinwood kids in the 1930s

thug). There is a photograph from the 1930s of my father, his twin sister, three brothers, and some unknown kid from the neighborhood (Figure 1.1). It is an image of streetwise comradery.

Those were close-knit immigrant neighborhoods, especially during hard times, and people stuck together, families helped other families. "I never knew we were poor," my mother always said, because everyone was the same. That's the story we were told. There is another one I heard only in the last month of her life, about the first house her father moved my mother and her three siblings into, with no running water and an infestation of rats.

We kids loved stories about the old neighborhood, where street characters and troublemakers had names like Snowball and Bad-Eye. As far back as I can remember, there has been a hand-painted

Figure 1.2 Wileman Foley Faience Decorative Plate, circa 1895

decorative plate hanging in the dining room of my parents' house. It depicts two curious people, one in a little cap sitting on a doorstep and one in a top hat standing on the road.[4] Written across the top of the picture are the words "THE ARTFUL DODGER AND OLIVER TWIST" and below it the caption "HULLO, MY COVEY : WHAT'S THE ROW!" (Figure 1.2). About four years ago I was chatting with my mother about nothing and asked her where she ever got that Artful Dodger plate. "Oh, that's so old," she said dismissively. "Bad-Eye's father took it out of the trash."

When my father died, I grieved because I loved him and knew how much I would miss him. I felt no ambivalence, he was a wonderful man to me, never a critical word, never a judgment. My relationship with my mother was more complicated. I am still dealing with her death, and I am still haunted by her. But there was never any question, ever, that my parents loved me. Love simply flowed from them, they were just so happy to have a family. They were simple people in that way. It was just parental love, unquestionable and solid as a rock, so absolutely normal no one had to declare it or make a fuss over it—I think we only started to say "I love you" to one another after Joseph died, and only on special occasions. The family, the family. Someone would always catch you, you supported one another, you sent birthday cards and accepted loans, you called your mother every Sunday. It was elementary, and it would always be there. Love, ordinary as rain.

"HULLO, MY COVEY : WHAT'S THE ROW!" is an odd phrase to have swimming in your mind all your life, but it has served as my own strange little mantra, the first words I knew by Charles Dickens, even before "Bah, Humbug!" In *Oliver Twist*, the Artful Dodger is introduced in Chapter 8, "Oliver Walks to London. He Encounters On The Road A Strange Sort of Young Gentleman." Here is the scene that is depicted on my decorative plate:

> [Oliver] had been crouching on the step for some time...gazing list-lessly at the coaches as they passed...when he was roused by observing that a boy, who had passed him carelessly some minutes before, had returned, and was now surveying him most earnestly from the opposite side of the way. He took little heed of this at first; but the boy remained in the same attitude of close observation so long, that Oliver raised his head, and returned his steady look. Upon this, the boy crossed over; and walking close up to Oliver, said,

"Hullo, my covey! What's the row?"

The boy who addressed this inquiry to the young wayfarer, was about his own age: but one of the queerest looking boys that Oliver had even seen. He was a snub-nosed, flat-browed, common-faced boy enough; and as dirty a juvenile as one would wish to see; but he had about him all the airs and manners of a man. He was short of his age: with rather bow-legs, and little, sharp, ugly eyes. His hat was stuck on the top of his head so lightly, that it threatened to fall off every moment—and would have done so, very often, if the wearer had not had a knack of every now and then giving his head a sudden twitch, which brought it back to its old place again. He wore a man's coat, which reached nearly to his heels. He had turned the cuffs back, half-way up his arm, to get his hands out of the sleeves: apparently with the ultimate view of thrusting them into the pockets of his corduroy trousers; for there he kept them. He was, altogether, as roystering and swaggering a young gentleman as ever stood four feet six, or something less, in the bluchers.

"Hullo, my covey! What's the row?" said this strange young gentleman to Oliver.[5]

A *covey*, by the way, is a small flock of birds, usually partridges. *Bluchers* are tie-up shoes, like oxfords. A *row* (rhymes with *ow!*) is a bit of trouble. *Roystering* (or *roistering*) is a splendid word: it means swaggering and acting boisterously.

The Dodger's strange and colorful vocabulary is world-expanding for little Oliver. He learns that words remake the everyday, multiplying its meanings—a *beak* can mean a magistrate *and* a bird's mouth. "*Beak's* order, eh?" "My *flash* com-pan-i-on." "My eyes, how *green!*" "The *mill* as takes up so little room that it'll work inside *a Stone Jug.*" "You want *grub*, and you shall have it. I'm at *low-water-mark* myself—only one *bob and a magpie*; but, as far as it goes, I'll *fork out and stump.* Up with you on your *pins.* There! Now then! '*Morrice!*'" (8). The Artful Dodger has the wit and audacity of one of Dickens's best creations, Sam Weller from *The Pickwick Papers*. Both characters have a style of speech that's all their own. As Ali Smith comments in her marvelous book, *Artful*, Dickens's novel comes newly alive with the Dodger's slang, because this is when Oliver begins to see life's richness and variety, and to interpret its possibilities.[6] You can feel 25-year-old Dickens getting warmed up when the Dodger makes his first appearance in *Oliver Twist*. Oliver learns from him that words have twists in their meanings and that people can have shifting identities. A dirty, common-faced boy can also be a little gentleman and flaunt a few different names—the Artful, Jack Dawkins, the Dodger. He has "a knack" for things, artfully balancing his hat on his head, keeping a ready-dressed ham clean by stuffing it into a loaf of bread, spotting a prime plant. And he straightaway gets Oliver some grub. "First feed the face, then talk right and wrong."[7] There are worse teachers in the school of life than the Artful. Lucky for Oliver he ran into him.

The decorative plate with the mysterious words "Hullo, my covey!" (now hanging in my own dining room) was all I knew of Dickens for most of my childhood. Until Lionel Bart's hit musical, *Oliver!* As far as I know, my father never saw *Oliver!* on any stage, though he owned the record from the 1960 London show. What he knew and loved was Carol Reed's 1968 Oscar-winning film, and so did I. We were fans. I even own the piano music for *Oliver!*, with black-and-white photo stills and a "Souvenir Folio containing all the songs in the motion picture." I think my father and I loved *Oliver!* because of the story and the songs, and its overall bright-ness and optimism, the energy of musical theater minimizing the horrors actually being depicted. I wonder now if I even knew that Nancy and Bet were prostitutes. But who knows why any work of art sticks to you. Maybe it was the Disneyfied Englishness of *Oliver!*

(the genesis, maybe, of my Anglophilia), or Fagin and the Artful Dodger, characters who seemed to me straight out of the Brothers Grimm. Maybe it was the ritual excitement of watching the movie with my father. His favorite line was Fagin's "Shut up and drink yer gin!"

I think I must see the actors from *Oliver!* in my dreams. I knew that film and all the songs by heart, and throughout my childhood and adolescence, I believed that *Oliver!* was the novel Dickens wrote. My father was not one for novels, and for years he shared my innocence—until I read *Oliver Twist*, and told him what really happens to Fagin. It was not the ending either of us wanted to believe.

Oliver Twist is one of the most dramatized of all Dickens's novels. It has been endlessly adapted—in the 1830s, it hit the stage about ten minutes after Dickens put down his pen. In *A Small Boy and Others*, Henry James recalls the sensational posters he saw in New York City for dramatic adaptations of Dickens's novels. He remembers going to see a performance of *Nicholas Nickleby* "that gracelessly managed to be all tearful melodrama" and cut out half the story. It was so awful, so subtractive, and yet James testifies to how Dickens's genius sticks even to bad theatrical adaptations:

> [I]n face of my sharp retention…through all the years who shall deny the immense authority of the theatre, or that the stage is the mightiest of modern engines? Such at least was to be the force of the Dickens imprint, however applied, in the soft clay of our generation; it was to resist so serenely the wash of the waves of time.[8]

In the next century, Dickens's imprint pressed even more firmly into collective consciousness through the engine of cinema. The first silent film adaptation of *Oliver Twist* was as early as 1909.

Dickens loved the theater, and he understood the power of images. He always had very careful instructions for his illustrators. Graham Greene thought the illustrations to Dickens's novels froze "the excited, excitable world of Dickens into a hall of waxworks." Brilliant as they were, Greene thought Phiz and Cruikshank "did Dickens a disservice, for no character any more will walk for the first time into our memory as we ourselves imagine him."[9] True enough. Henry James recalled that *Oliver Twist* "seemed to me more Cruikshank's than Dickens's; it was a thing of such vividly terrible images."[10] In my imagination, Oliver Twist has Mark Lester's face, and my Fagin is without a doubt Ron Moody. Images for *Oliver Twist* have been commodified and circulated for more than a century—witness my Artful Dodger plate. In England in the 1930s, for example, there was a Terry's chocolate bar called Oliver Twist. The wrapper depicted a well-dressed, rosy-cheeked boy holding out a bowl, one of hundreds of spinoffs of Cruikshank's iconic illustration from 1837. The memory of that chocolate wrapper stayed with Lionel Bart into adulthood. He claimed that "the image for the show came to me from a candy."[11]

The earliest things in life—kitsch, candy wrappers, popular music—become associated over time with such complex emotions and memories. The songs in *Oliver!* at different times can revive in me feelings of joy or attachment, sadness or loss. It's all gone, the 60s, my childhood, my father's pure delight at Fagin's "Reviewing the Situation," Nancy's "Ohm-Pah-Pah," and especially the beautifully choreographed "Who Will Buy," his favorite number. All his life, my father talked about a high-school class he had in music theory. This would have been in the 1930s, when he played the clarinet in the Collinwood High School band. He never had a chance to study theory or play his clarinet much after that, but music remained a passion and a pleasure. In the 1970s, when I was in high school, every Saturday morning at nine o'clock we listened together to "Adventures in Good Music" on WCLV radio, with the great and sonorous Karl Haas. After my father retired, he put on a classical cd after breakfast every morning, sat in his chair in the living room, and listened. He loved Italian opera, Beethoven's symphonies, patriotic marches, and big band music—straightforward styles, big styles, nothing too avant-garde, just as he did not like movies with ambiguous endings and layers of irony. "Just tell the story!" he always said. When he was in the nursing home and showing signs of dementia, I brought him a boombox and a double-cd collection entitled *Those Were Our Songs: Music of World War II*. Though his memory had been slipping, he remembered almost all of those obscure songs, the melody, the words, the vocalists, even the bandleaders. We listened together to some of the corniest music I've ever heard, "Praise the Lord and Pass the Ammunition," "Mairzy Doats," "Shoo-Shoo Baby." But, also, some of the greatest—sentimental songs about saying goodbye and being far away, songs about love and longing for home. My father knew those songs after more than 50 years, because they were still inside of him.

There is a scene in *Oliver!* when Oliver has his first night in the thieves' den. It is after the boys play the pickpocket game. Fagin has made everyone go to bed, and Oliver asks meekly, "Where do I sleep, sir?" Fagin takes Oliver apart from the others and puts him in a tattered basket around the corner. He takes off the boy's ragged boots and covers him with a blanket. For a few seconds, longer than the story seems to require, the camera lingers on the actors' faces in close-up. It is disconcerting. Is Fagin hatching an evil plot? Or does Oliver's purity touch something human in him? Fagin whispers, slowly, pausingly, "If you go on the way you started, you will be the greatest man of all time. Sweet dreams, Oliver. Sweet dreams." And weary little Oliver gazes with bewildered gratitude on the old man who has fed him and amused him and made him ready for bed. "Good night, sir," he says, politely. Fagin and Oliver look at one another again, then Fagin softly sings the chorus from "You've Got to Pick a Pocket or Two" until we see Oliver close his eyes and fall asleep.[12]

This segment has been referred to as "the lullaby scene," and several film critics cited it at the time of *Oliver!*'s release as one of the most significant moments in the film. Joseph Gelmis wrote in *Newsday*, "Suddenly, like a revelation, [Fagin's] passive, thoughtful expression imperceptibly seemed to be the tender look of a man tucking his child into bed for the night. And the tone of the film was set in a poignant flash: Fagin was a father figure to this troop of little lost beggars."[13] As it happens, this was exactly right. Lionel Bart wrote to Ron Moody in 1960 that among the four main threads of the story as he conceived it was that "of a lonely Jew who is searching for love, and finds it from the children he fosters."[14] In the fond looks, the teasing, the gin-and-water, the slapping around, there's a curious amalgam of attachment between Fagin and the boys.

> BOYS
> How could we forget
> How could we let
> Our dear old Fagin worry?
> We love him so.
> We'll come back home
> In, oh, such a great big
> Hurry . . .

FAGIN
Cheerio, but be back soon.
I dunno, somehow I'll miss you
I love you, that why I
Say, "Cheerio"
Not goodbye…[15]

Don't stay out too late! says Fagin. We won't, don't worry! say the boys. Familial, familiar, routine. Love, ordinary as rain.

Oliver's theme song, "Where Is Love?" is the centerpiece of Lionel Bart's musical. "All the other songs in the show belong to that song," Bart said. "Musically, it's the root theme for the rest of the songs." Later in his career he reflected, "I like to believe it is a song about what Charles Dickens was looking for in his life."[16] Charles Dickens and Lionel Bart were able to imagine Oliver's loneliness with such intensity because they knew what it meant to feel forsaken, to be on the outside instead of the inside. Dickens both saw and felt the indifference of most of society to any one small person's hurt. So did Lionel Bart. He was "a cockney-Jewish East Ender," the youngest of seven surviving children, born in 1930 to Jewish refugees from Austria-Hungary.[17] His father was a tailor. Though he wrote the music, the lyrics, and the book for *Oliver!* Bart did not have an advanced education, and no formal schooling at all in music. The melodic simplicity of most of the songs in *Oliver!* came from the English music hall tradition; Fagin's songs came from Jewish klezmer music. Bart's formative years were spent in Brick Lane and Stepney Way, and his creative energies came from the speech and culture of working-class people. Like Dickens, he did not write down to these people; he wrote for them. Ron Moody thought that some day Bart would be acknowledged "as one of the great folk composers of his day."[18] Bart's 1999 obituary in *The Guardian* noted that he "was his 46-year-old mother's eleventh child and attributed his desire for fame to what he felt had been a lack of love and attention from his overworked, and older than average, parents."[19] "Where Is Love?", the harmonic ballad that Bart said anchored the play, expresses feelings that go back to Bart's roots and to a desire for acceptance—the "lonely Jew who is searching for love." Oliver's theme song may be about what Dickens was looking for, but it was also about Lionel Bart.

Dickens wrote in his 1841 Preface to the novel, "I wished to show, in little Oliver the principle of Good surviving through every adverse circumstance, and triumphing at last." Yet there is something very serious and unsettling at the root of *Oliver Twist*. We tend to forget a disturbing scene early in the novel, when Oliver is newly apprenticed to Mr. Sowerberry. He is taken to the home of a poor woman who has died. The woman's elderly mother is demented, and her husband is crazed with grief. When Sowerberry goes down on his knees to measure the body for her coffin, the husband rages at the irony:

> "Ah!" said the man: bursting into tears, and sinking on his knees at the feet of the dead woman; "kneel down, kneel down—kneel round her, every one of you, and mark my words! I say she was starved to death. I never knew how bad she was, till the fever came upon her; and then her bones were starting through the skin. There was neither fire nor candle; she died in the dark—in the dark! She couldn't even see her children's faces, though we heard her gasping out their names. I begged for her in the streets: and they sent me to prison. When I came back, she was dying; and all the blood in my heart has dried up, for they starved her to death. I swear it before the God that saw it! They starved her!" He twined his hands in his hair; and, with a loud scream, rolled grovelling upon the floor: his eyes fixed, and the foam covering his lips. (5)

The next day at the burial, neighborhood boys jump back and forth over the coffin until the grave-digger fills up the hole, "no very difficult task, for the grave was so full, that the uppermost coffin was within a few feet of the surface." He stamps it down and walks away. (That overflowing grave stayed in Dickens's inner eye, by the way—in *Bleak House*, Nemo's corpse is taken to "a hemmed-in churchyard, pestiferous and obscene" and lowered down "a foot or two."[20]) The husband falls down in a swoon, Sowerberry throws a can of cold water over him, and the ritual is done. These miserable people never re-enter the story. They don't even have names. The narration is determinedly cold.

> "Well, Oliver," said Sowerberry, as they walked home, "how do you like it?"
>
> "Pretty well, thank you, sir," replied Oliver, with considerable hesitation. "Not very much, sir."
>
> "Ah, you'll get used to it in time, Oliver," said Sowerberry. "Nothing when you *are* used to it, my boy." (5)

This is 13 years before *Bleak House*, and it is as dark as anything Dickens writes about the material, mental, and emotional sufferings of the poor.

John Bayley has written that *Oliver Twist* makes "a piercing appeal to something private and vulnerable in the memory of the reader."[21] It seems to touch a hidden need. Bart placed his finger on the wound when he made "Where Is Love?" the heart of his play. And despite its cheerful revisionism, I think *Oliver!* got this right. Victorian sentimentality and the sentimentality of musical theater cannot rub out Dickens's insight, at the age of 25, into the devastation of lovelessness, how emotionally and spiritually bereft people were in his society, despite all that middle-class Bible reading. David Lean made a brilliant decision when he had the workhouse plastered with Biblical platitudes in his 1948 film: GOD IS GOOD. GOD IS JUST. GOD IS LOVE. Carol Reed's *Oliver!* has GOD IS LOVE in giant letters on the workhouse walls, a completely meaningless abstraction for the illiterate and starving orphans. In *Oliver Twist*, Bumble remarks proudly that "the porochial seal" is a cast of "the Good Samaritan healing the sick and bruised man." (4) "I hope you say your prayers every night," one gruff old member of the board tells Oliver, "and pray for the people who feed you, and take care of you—like a Christian." (2) It's really the hypocrisy Dickens despises.

Graham Greene thought that in *Oliver Twist* Dickens created a world without God, a Manichean world that seems almost to have been invented by Satan.[22] It is a world where everyone is on their own from day one, where no one can take for granted that they are loved or deserve to be loved, where people are commodities and every feeling is a matter of exchange and barter. Dickens did not invent this nightmare. It was what England felt like after 1834. Dickens's attacks on the workhouse system and the Poor Law are scathing:

> The members of this board were very sage, deep, philosophical men; and when they came to turn their attention to the workhouse, they found out at once, what ordinary folks would never have discovered—the poor people liked it! It was a regular place of public entertainment for the poorer classes; a tavern where there was nothing to pay; a public breakfast, dinner, tea, and supper all the year round; a brick and mortar elysium, where it was all play and no work. "Oho!" said the board, looking very knowing; "we are the fellows to set this to rights; we'll stop it all, in no time." So, they established the rule, that all poor people should have the alternative (for they would compel nobody, not they), of being starved by a gradual process in the house, or by a quick one out of it. . . .

For the first six months after Oliver Twist was removed, the system was in full operation. It was rather expensive at first, in consequence of the increase in the undertaker's bill, and the necessity of taking in the clothes of all the paupers, which fluttered loosely on their wasted, shrunken forms, after a week or two's gruel. But the number of workhouse inmates got thin as well as the paupers; and the board were in ecstasies. (2)

When Oliver asks for more, he's treated like a criminal and "ordered into instant confinement."

For a week after the commission of the impious and profane offence of asking for more, Oliver remained a close prisoner in the dark and solitary room to which he had been consigned by the wisdom and mercy of the board. It appears, at first sight not unreasonable to suppose, that, if he had entertained a becoming feeling of respect for the prediction of the gentleman in the white waistcoat, he would have established that sage individual's prophetic character, once and for ever, by tying one end of his pocket-handkerchief to a hook in the wall, and attaching himself to the other. To the performance of this feat, however, there was one obstacle: namely, that pocket-handkerchiefs being decided articles of luxury, had been, for all future times and ages, removed from the noses of paupers by the express order of the board, in council assembled: solemnly given and pronounced under their hands and seals. (2)

This, by the way is the first mention of pocket-handkerchiefs in *Oliver Twist*. A pocket-handkerchief is an item of luxury that someone might want to pinch. It may also be used as an improvised noose. Clever of Dickens to see that.

Fear of abandonment, an inescapable sense of isolation, anxiety and uncertainty about tomorrow, and complete dependence on the adult officials in charge: this is the overwhelming reality for Oliver. At Mrs. Mann's farm, at Mr. Sowerberry's, at the Workhouse, in Fagin's den, Oliver is confined in dark, small, windowless places. My mind went to Dickens as I read about the hundreds of children who were separated from their parents at the U.S.–Mexico border during the Trump administration, confined in what some reporters called concentration camps. A lawyer who visited the detention centers in Texas said, "[O]ne of the children described as many as three hundred children being in that room, in that warehouse. . . . There were no windows."[23]

When there is no God, no mother, when there is nothing at all to begin from, people will take whatever love they can find. In Chapter 4, Bumble is taking Oliver to Mr. Sowerberry's:

Although Oliver did as he was desired, at once; and passed the back of his unoccupied hand briskly across his eyes, he left a tear in them when he looked up at his conductor. As Mr. Bumble gazed sternly upon him, it rolled down his cheek. It was followed by another, and another. The child made a strong effort, but it was an unsuccessful one. Withdrawing his other hand from Mr. Bumble's he covered his face with both; and wept until the tears sprang from between his chin and bony fingers.

"Well!" exclaimed Mr. Bumble, stopping short, and darting at his little charge a look of intense malignity. "Well! Of *all* the ungratefullest, and worst-disposed boys as ever I see, Oliver, you are the—"

"No, no, sir," sobbed Oliver, clinging to the hand which held the well-known cane; "no, no, sir; I will be good indeed; indeed I will, sir! I am a very little boy, sir; and it is so—so—"

"So what?" inquired Mr. Bumble in amazement.

"So lonely, sir! So very lonely!" cried the child. "Everybody hates me. Oh! sir, don't, don't pray be cross to me!" The child beat his hand upon his heart; and looked in his companion's face, with tears of real agony.

Mr. Bumble regarded Oliver's piteous and helpless look, with some astonishment, for a few seconds; hemmed three or four times in a husky manner; and after muttering something about "that troublesome cough," bade Oliver dry his eyes and be a good boy. Then once more taking his hand, he walked on with him in silence. (4)

Dry your eyes, be a good lad, take my hand. Bumble's tiny, tiny impulse toward something like paternal care undermines his heartless buffoonery for just a moment when he regards Oliver's tears of agony. The two of them almost seem like a strict father and a sensitive son. The beadle was a looming presence in Oliver's very early childhood. He gave Oliver his ingenious name. He is taking him to be apprenticed to a stranger, a coffin-maker named Mr. Sowerberry. The beadle is all Oliver has. Is it any surprise that as they walk along Oliver *clings* to the hand that carries the whip?

We take love wherever and whenever it is offered, in whatever guise, in authoritarianism, in food or drink, in money, in sex, in crime. Nancy tells Rose Maylie, "When such as I...set our rotten hearts on any man, and let him fill the place that has been a blank through all our wretched lives, who can hope to cure us? Pity us, lady—pity us for having only one feeling of the woman left, and for having that turned, by a heavy judgment, from a comfort and a pride, into a new means of violence and suffering."(40) "Who else would love him still / When they've been used so ill?" Nancy sings, in her signature ballad, "As Long As He Needs Me." Love is in such tragically scarce supply in this novel. Everyone is asking for more.

Dickens's celebration of the family unit in all his novels may have been psychological compensation for his own experience of early abandonment. Or, it could just be a Victorian convention, the so-called genealogical imperative. The good people wind up married, with a cottage garden and a brood of children to secure the future for England. Politically alert readers have been bothered by this withdrawal into middle-class safety, Dickens's tendency to create what Bert Hornback has evocatively called "pockets of love."[24]

Oliver Twist ends this way, with the "little society" of good people safe in their happy village refuge. Yet what about the vital and active love needed to keep the world from devolving into chaos? What about humanitarian love?

Oliver Twist is a novel about not having parents, not having anyone you can call your people. Family life is a makeshift arrangement. There are virtually no intact or consanguineous families in *Oliver Twist* (this is also striking in *David Copperfield*, where David, Steerforth, Agnes, Annie, and Dora have lost a parent, and Ham, Em'ly, Traddles, and Martha are orphans). Monks is only Oliver's half-brother, Rose is his maternal aunt. Mr. Brownlow is a bachelor with a live-in housekeeper; Mr. Grimwig seems to have no relations at all. Mrs. Maylie is a widow who took pity on Rose when she was a miserable orphan and adopted her. Bumble, with mercenary motives, marries the widow Mrs. Corney, but starting a family is the last thing on his mind. Fagin, as we've seen, is a kind of foster parent to Charley Bates and the Dodger, but of unknown origins. (Everyone is of unknown origins except, eventually, Oliver, Monks, and Rose.) Sikes and Nancy are an unmarried couple who co-habit and apparently share their earnings, but all is not right in that relationship, obviously. Mr. and Mrs. Sowerberry are sour and childless (unless Charlotte is their daughter, but that's never clear). Noah Claypole is a charity-boy, not an orphan, but Dickens makes his own ironic point about his antecedents: "No chance-child was he, for he could trace his genealogy all the way back to his parents, who lived hard by; his mother being a washerwoman, and his father a drunken soldier, discharged with a wooden leg, and a diurnal pension of twopence-halfpenny and an unstateable fraction." (5) And the orphans in the workhouse? They have their guardians and surrogates, the "kind and blessed gentleman which is so many parents to you, Oliver, when you have none of your own," as Bumble says. They "are a going to 'prentice you: and to set you up in life, and make a man of you: although the expense to the parish is three pound ten!—three pound ten, Oliver!—seventy shillins—one hundred and forty sixpences!—and all for a naughty orphan which nobody can't love." (3)

Almost every domestic arrangement in *Oliver Twist* is provisional or a matter of barter and trade. People live in communal hives, the workhouse, the baby farm, Fagin's den (it's always a "den" for Fagin), where kids are picked off the street. Or else they live in protected private houses with people not related to them. "Consider Yourself at Home!" is a bitter refrain for children who are homeless or adopted. Yet each of these improvised human arrangements has its own rituals and assigned roles. People form bonds which have an emotional logic of their own.

In *Oliver!* there is a brief scene where Nancy (Shani Wallis) is frying up breakfast while Sikes (Oliver Reed) lies in bed in the dingy room they share. It's early in the morning. Sikes wants her to shut up about breakfast so he can get some sleep. (Nancy, sweetly obliging, says "I'll warm it up for your supper.") On her way out to get the money Fagin owes them, she pauses to look affectionately at Sikes. Her theme, "As Long As He Needs Me," plays softly in the background. "Bill," she says, leaning on the bedrail, "You do love, me don't you?" He sits up in bed in total male annoyance—he's had a long night of housebreaking—and growls, "Of course I do. I live with you, don't I?" and flops back down to sleep. Nancy smiles. She beams. Bill loves her. She skips away. At the end of the scene we see that Sikes's dog, Bull's-Eye, is cozily asleep at the foot of his master's bed.

In *Oliver Twist*, Sikes murders Nancy in that room. It is the central, riveting action of the novel, Dickens's first treatment of death through violent crime, and his first attempt to enter the subjectivity of a murderer. The murder scene in *Oliver Twist* obsessed Dickens throughout his career—the "Murder" was the most thrilling, famous, and physically demanding of his public readings. But Nancy's murder as Dickens wrote it was too graphic for Reed's musical: in *Oliver!* Sikes clubs Nancy to death behind a wall by the bridge where she met with Mr. Brownlow. The blood and gore are left to our imaginations. Dickens, though, describes the murder of Nancy with chilling deliberation and great artistry. I will admit, when I first read *Oliver Twist* as a young adult I was *shocked* by the murder scene (I see the same reaction in college students when I teach the novel). A Victorian reader's response to Nancy's murder must have been disturbingly intense. Dickens's handling of the murder and its aftermath was unlike anything his readers would have found in the Newgate novels of the 1830s. When he performed the Murder in his public readings, people screamed with terror. Women had to be carried out of the auditorium.

Dickens sets the scene cinematically: light and dark imagery dominate (David Lean's *Oliver Twist* effectively honors Dickens's dramatic strategy). The crime occurs "two hours before daybreak; that time, which, in the autumn of the year, may be truly called the dead of night." When Sikes gets to their room, he extinguishes a burning candle by throwing it into the grate, and Nancy, "seeing the faint light of day" gets up and tries to open the curtain. "There's light enough for wot I've got to do," Sikes snarls. After the first blow, he covers his eyes with his hand to avoid seeing Nancy's bloody figure, and in a blind rage, strikes her repeatedly: "with terror added to hate, he struck and struck again." Then it's daybreak.

The brilliant sun "burst upon the crowded city in clear and radiant glory. Through the costly-coloured glass and paper-mended window, through cathedral dome and rotten crevice, it shed its equal ray. It lighted up the room where the murdered woman lay. It did." The ordinariness of the new day, the carelessness of it, magnifies the horror of Sikes's act. The "pool of gore . . . quivered and danced in the sunlight on the ceiling," "the sun poured down upon the very spot!" Sikes strikes a light in order to destroy the weapon, and the flame further illuminates the room. He had to turn away from Nancy during the actual murder, but now that she is dead, he is drawn obsessively to the corpse. He watches her hair on the end of the club blaze up and keeps his grasp on it until it breaks, he looks at the blood stains on his clothing, on the floor, even on the dog's feet, while "All of this time he had, never once, turned his back upon the corpse." (47) After the murder, with the sun streaming in, the body is so dreadful to behold that Sikes throws a rug over it. But it is worse to *imagine* the expressionless eyes, so he plucks it off again. Then, he stares at the body: "mere flesh and blood, no more—but such flesh, and so much blood!" (48) We later learn that Nancy's body is so horribly mutilated that when the prostitute Bet is brought to identify it, she has to be taken away in a straitjacket. (50)

Some readers have felt that after the murder Sikes becomes a tragic figure. Garry Wills, for instance, noted that Nancy's murder "stirs in the inert stuff of Sikes [a] belated recognition of his love for her. . . . The wrench of Nancy's loss leaves Sikes bewildered by the beginnings of human feeling in him."[25] As he plunges into the dark and solitary road, away from people and towns, he is haunted by "that morning's ghastly figure following at his heels," no longer a woman, only an "it."

At times, he turned, with desperate determination, resolved to beat this phantom off, though it should look him dead; but the hair rose on his head, and his blood stood still, for it had turned with him and was behind him then. He had kept it before him that morning, but it was behind now—always. He leaned his back against a bank, and felt that it stood above him, visibly out against the cold night-sky. He threw himself upon the road—on his back upon the road. At his head it stood, silent, erect, and still—a living grave-stone, with its epitaph in blood. (48)

"Let no man talk of murderers escaping justice," Dickens writes, "and hint that Providence must sleep. There were twenty score of violent deaths in one long minute of that agony of fear." (48) What Sikes suffers is more than guilt, more than the apprehension of being caught and hanged. Sikes knows in the pit of his heart that he is now totally cut off, morally alone in the universe. Like men before and since, he has killed the only person in the world who loved him.

> "Why does your sword so drip with blood,
> Edward, Edward?
> Why does your sword so drip with blood?
> And why so sad are ye, O?"
> "O, I have killed my hawk so good,
> Mother, mother:
> O I have killed my hawk so good:
> And I had no more but he, O."[26]

Where is love? There is no denying that people are very, very cruel in *Oliver Twist*. Mrs. Mann the baby-farmer locks children in a dark coal-cellar. The magistrate Fang, whom Dickens based on a notorious judge, is a lawful dictator. Maybe he is a suffering soul inside, but Dickens really hates him. "Yet, dotted everywhere / Ironic

points of light / Flash out wherever the Just / Exchange their mes-
sages."[27] People are not without compassion. There is the surgeon
when Oliver is born, who consoles his mother "with more kindness than might have been expected of him." (1) There is the magistrate with the tortoise-shell spectacles who by chance sees
Oliver's "pale and terrified" face at the prospect of being apprenticed to evil Mr. Gamfield the chimney-sweep, and refuses to sign
the indentures. (3) On his seven-day journey to London, there is a
"good-hearted turnpike man" who gives Oliver a meal of bread
and cheese, and a "benevolent old lady" with "a shipwrecked
grandson wandering barefoot in some distant part of the earth,"
who pities Oliver and gives him the little she can afford "with such
kind and gentle words, and such tears of sympathy and compassion, that they sank deeper into Oliver's soul, than all the sufferings he had ever undergone." (8) There is the "kind-hearted
thief-taker" in Fang's courtroom who stoops down to ask his
name, and the absent-minded bookstall-keeper who rushes to the
magistrate's office to vindicate Oliver just as he is being dragged
off to his cell. (11) There is the officer in Fagin's condemned cell
who holds Oliver by the hand and whispers to him not to be
afraid. (52) Love by committee doesn't help Oliver. But these
nameless, more than minor characters tell me that all is not lost.
There are a lot of incompetent caregivers and representatives of
the law in *Oliver Twist*, but at least a half-blind magistrate recog-
nizes a terrified child when he sees one. At least an underling of
Fang's can try to protect a helpless orphan from three months of
hard labor.

There is also little Dick, the orphan Oliver befriends at Mrs.
Mann's baby farm. It's easy to forget about this character, but he is

a very important point of hope (his name anticipates benevolent, scatterbrained Mr. Dick in *David Copperfield*). Dick had been Oliver's "little friend and playmate. They had been beaten, and starved, and shut up together, many and many a time." (7) Dick's innate Christian charity is a slap in the face to the "porochial seal"—he reminds me of Helen Burns in *Jane Eyre* in his mute endurance of injustice. When Oliver passes Mrs. Mann's cottage after he escapes from Mr. Sowerberry's, he sees Dick weeding in the garden.

> "Kiss me," said the child, climbing up the low gate, and flinging his little arms round Oliver's neck. "Good-b'ye, dear! God bless you!"
>
> The blessing was from a young child's lips, but it was the first that Oliver had ever heard invoked upon his head; and through the struggles and sufferings, and troubles and changes, of his after life, he never once forgot it. (7)

And Oliver does *not* forget. When he is walking from Clerkenwell to return Mr. Brownlow's books, he thinks "how happy and contented he ought to feel; and how much he would give for only one look at poor little Dick, who, starved and beaten, might be weeping bitterly at that very moment." (15) Hoping to see Dick again when he returns to the place of his birth, Oliver tells Rose, "He said 'God bless you' to me when I ran away, and I will say 'God bless you' now, and show him how I love him for it!" (51) Nor does Dick forget Oliver. "I should like," he tells Bumble, "to leave my dear love to poor Oliver Twist; and to let him know how often I have sat by myself and cried to think of his wandering about in the dark nights with nobody to help him." (42) Under the existing system, the love between these two doomed outcasts is beyond logic, it is even radical. Instead of competing with one another for limited resources, that crust of bread or drop of water, Oliver and

Dick form a bond, a brotherhood. Dick's love remains an anchor of hope for Oliver. It's a slender thread, but Dickens understood how people hold on to the chance that a wrong can be made right, that victims will find justice and solace in the end. Oliver has an extravagant fantasy: he will rescue Dick from the baby farm, adopt him, take him to live with his new friends, the Maylies. It was not to be. "It is a world of disappointment: often to the hopes we most cherish, and hopes that do our nature the greatest honour." (52) Oliver's love for Dick, and Dick's love for Oliver, blesses them both. Even more, as Dickens makes clear, their *hope* for each other ennobles them.

Oliver's search, supposedly, is for maternal love. He does not want love in the abstract, and he does not want the warped humanitarianism of his official guardians. Oliver demands from the world the basic need of every human being. That first attachment is deep-rooted, it is in our bodies and our dreams. Our simplest gestures reveal it. As Oliver's mother lies dying in the workhouse, she "stretched out her hand towards the child. The surgeon deposited it in her arms. She imprinted her cold white lips passionately on its forehead." (1) When Oliver lies ill in bed at Mr. Brownlow's, Mrs. Bedwin "very gently placed Oliver's head upon the pillow; and, smoothing back his hair from his forehead, looked so kindly and lovingly in his face, that he could not help placing his little withered hand in hers, and drawing it round his neck." (12)

> "Save us!" said the old lady, with tears in her eyes. "What a grateful little dear it is. Pretty creetur! What would his mother feel if she had sat by him as I have, and could see him now!"
>
> "Perhaps she does see me," whispered Oliver, folding his hands together; "perhaps she has sat by me. I almost feel as if she had."

"That was the fever, my dear," said the old lady mildly.

"I suppose it was," replied Oliver, "because heaven is a long way off; and they are too happy there, to come down to the bedside of a poor boy. But if she knew I was ill, she must have pitied me, even there; for she was very ill herself before she died. She can't know anything about me though," added Oliver after a moment's silence. "If she had seen me hurt, it would have made her sorrowful; and her face has always looked sweet and happy, when I have dreamed of her." (12)

Again, when Rose Maylie sees Oliver after the burglary she "gathered Oliver's hair from his face. As she stooped over him, her tears fell upon his forehead." (30) Her gestures open Wordsworthian vistas:

The boy stirred, and smiled in his sleep, as though these marks of pity and compassion had awakened some pleasant dream of a love and affection he had never known. Thus, a strain of gentle music, or the rippling of water in a silent place, or the odour of a flower, or the mention of a familiar word, will sometimes call up sudden dim remembrances of scenes that never were, in this life; which vanish like a breath; which some brief memory of a happier existence, long gone by, would seem to have awakened; which no voluntary exertion of the mind can ever recall. (30)

"Where is love?" Oliver sings in the film. "Where is she / who I close my eyes / to see?" Dreams of love are deep inside Oliver. They rise to the surface through these acts of womanly tenderness. Is love, or the dream of love, something we comprehend prior to being born? "O joy! that in our embers / Is something that doth live, / That Nature yet remembers / What was so fugitive!"[28] John Forster claimed Dickens had no affection for Wordsworth, but other sources affirm that by 1839 Dickens had spoken admiringly of the poet.[29] In Chapter 32, Dickens writes:

The memories which peaceful country scenes call up, are not of this world, nor of its thoughts and hopes. . . . beneath all this, there lingers, in the least reflective mind, a vague and half-formed consciousness of having held such feelings long before, in some remote and distant time, which calls up solemn thoughts of distant times to come, and bends down pride and worldliness beneath it. (32)

Of course, not everyone in *Oliver Twist* seems to have had a harmonious pre-existence. Steven Marcus thought this "foretaste of heaven" was something Dickens had to invent, that the dreadful years when his parents moved the family to London had wiped from his memory the earlier, happy time among the country lanes of Chatham.[30] (It is on the narrow streets of Chatham that little David Copperfield encounters that "old monster," the horrible "goroogoroo!" man who cheats him of his jacket.) Being sent away to work at Warren's Blacking taught Dickens a lesson he never forgot, that love is provisional and precarious. When Oliver, in a half-awake trance, sees Fagin and Monks outside the Maylies' window "their look was as firmly impressed upon his memory, as if it had been deeply carved in stone, and set before him from his birth." (34) His prelapsarian dreams are undermined by the permanent imprint of those diabolical faces. Marcus connects this moment in the novel to Dickens's memory of being put on display in a window at Warren's Blacking, where passers-by could see him in his degradation. The private wound becomes the eternal, Manichean struggle of *Oliver Twist* as Graham Greene imagined it, "the nightmare fight between the darkness where the demons walk and the sunlight where the ineffectual goodness makes its last stand in a condemned world." Whatever Dickens's intentions, it is the scheming, malignant faces outside the window that "remain part of our imaginations forever."[31]

Where is love? An adult smooths a child's hair, carries him on his shoulders, leads him by the hand. These elemental gestures stir a protective instinct in most people—maybe when we see them, we commune with our own lost innocence, our primitive need to trust? At nine years old, Oliver is "a pale thin child, somewhat diminutive in stature, and decidedly small in circumference." (2) He's sensitive. He cries easily and is frequently faint. People have to lift him up or take him by the hand—Mr. Bumble often does so. On their way to the burglary, Sikes holds out his hand and Oliver takes it "mechanically." (22) Several times Nancy catches "the hand which Oliver instinctively placed in hers." (22) The Artful Dodger "firmly" takes Oliver's hand when they arrive at the thieves' den, and he even "smoothed Oliver's hair over his eyes" when he presents him to Fagin. (9) The instinct is there, the reflex to care for a helpless being—until something in life, personal trauma, neglect, just the way society is organized, spoils and annihilates that impulse.

Some of Dickens's contemporaries couldn't believe an orphan brought up in the workhouse would speak quite so correctly and express such genteel ideas. Readers also refused to accept Nancy's "fine sentiments" and "fine English." Dickens defended her: "there is not one word exaggerated or over-wrought. It is emphatically God's truth, for it is the truth he leaves in such depraved and miserable breasts; the hope yet lingering behind; the last fair drop of water at the bottom of the weed-choked well." (Preface) The *hope* to do good lingers even in a lost soul like Nancy, who sacrifices her life in service to that hope. It may be hard to believe, but Dickens insisted on it. "It is useless to discuss whether the conduct and character of the girl seems natural or unnatural, probable or improbable, right or wrong. IT IS TRUE." (Preface) But what about

Bill Sikes? Something must have happened to him to have made him so "utterly and incurably bad." "Whether every gentler human feeling is dead within such bosoms, or the proper chord to strike has rusted and is hard to find, I do not pretend to know." (Preface) This is a poetic way of admitting how impossible it is to understand bad people. A witness at one of the detention centers on the Texas border admitted as much:

> "I'm not going to say that most of the guards care about the kids, because we didn't talk to most of the guards, but I do believe in the inherent goodness of people. And when I've talked to guards, they seemed caring, and they had guards who, when the children were there for these very lengthy interviews, would bring the children lunches in the conference room. They're terrible lunches. That's how some of the guards are, but the fact is that some of the guards are bad people, and there's no question about it."[32]

It can indeed be hard to find the rusted chord of human sympathy within some people, very hard.

Looking out for number one is the creed of both pickpockets and capitalists, then and now. Yet in *Oliver Twist*, Dickens leaves an opening to at least imagine that the natural movement of our hearts is not toward self-preservation alone. It is not just a battle against a cold, indifferent universe or a tribal enemy. There is still Nancy, who risks her life for Oliver for reasons she herself does not understand. She has been taught that sympathy is a weakness, that you have to be tough as nails to survive. When she goes to see Rose Maylie, Dickens writes, ". . . even this degraded being felt too proud to betray a feeble gleam of the womanly feeling which she thought a weakness, but which alone connected her with that humanity, of which her wasting life had obliterated so many, many traces when a very child." (40) In the scene between Rose and Nancy, the fallen woman and the pure angel, Dickens identifies sad social realities, profound social and psychological truths. Both women realize with horror and grace the precarity of life, and they see what immeasurably divides them. But they also see what connects them, as vulnerable women and as human beings.

When Rose offers her money, Nancy refuses. Given the way people are consistently utilized and commodified in *Oliver Twist*, this is a huge gesture, an awakening. Nancy has just stepped onto a greater moral stage. Rose implores Nancy, "Think once again on your own condition, and the opportunity you have of escaping from it. You have a claim on me: not only as the voluntary bearer of this intelligence, but as a woman lost almost beyond redemption.... Oh! is there no chord in your heart that I can touch! Is there nothing left, to which I can appeal against this terrible infatuation!" The rusted chord is in Nancy, too, in her terrible infatuation, in her blindness to her own brave potential. Rose too is incredibly brave. To say to a prostitute, "You have a claim on me," is to refuse the artificial laws of her society and instead follow the model of Christ. Nancy replies, "...dear, sweet, angel lady, you *are* the first that ever blessed me with such words as these, and if I had heard them years ago, they might have turned me from a life of sin and sorrow; but it is too late, it is too late!" (46) When she meets Rose and Brownlow on London Bridge, Nancy again refuses to take Rose's purse. "I have not done this for money," she insists. "Let me have that to think of." Mr. Brownlow wants to find a safe asylum for her in England or abroad where she can start a new life. But Nancy refuses. "I am chained to my old life. I loathe and hate it now, but I cannot leave it. I must have gone too far to turn back,— and yet I don't know, for if you had spoken to me so, some time ago, I should have laughed it off." (46) Something has changed for

Nancy. Was it something in Oliver's bewildered, frightened face? Her pity for him forced her to act. But perhaps there was also something in her conversation with Rose. For after that meeting, Nancy has to face a terrible self-knowledge. She is no longer defiantly proud to be a lost woman, her life is not glamorously free and rebellious. That was all a lie, a show in a music hall, a song and dance. Now she understands exactly what has been taken from her and how her need for love has been debased and perverted. She will not let the same thing happen to Oliver.

Though Nancy will not take money, she wants a token of love, and gratefully accepts Rose's white handkerchief. Nancy will take this handkerchief from her bosom and raise it up to God after she is bludgeoned by Sikes. "Bless you! God bless you!" she whispers to Rose on the bridge. Thank you for trusting me, for seeing that I'm a human being, for pitying me. For helping me, in this last desperate act of my wasted life, to move closer to the Good.

My father was the kind of person who always earnestly said thank you, even for the smallest thing. One kind word or gesture from a clerk, a nurse, a patient, a visitor, a janitor, a housekeeper, brought from him humility and gratitude. "Thank you *very very* much," he said, and he always meant it. When I hear myself saying these words, I know exactly where they come from. Of course, when they were in nursing homes, both my father and mother also said, repeatedly and repeatedly, those other words, less humble but just as sincere: "I'm going home!" As grateful as they were for the care of kind and competent medical professionals, they were getting out of there.

I spent two and a half weeks in Cleveland in July and August of 2019, that summer my mother was shuttled between hospitals and nursing homes. Two and a half weeks is not a long time—I see now it was not nearly long enough—but it felt long to me. I would get up every morning and float my parents' Buick through the dreary suburbs to the hospital to sit with my mother all day. Although it was what I wanted to do and where I wanted to be, the eight hours I spent in her room, sitting on a hard chair, waiting for something to happen—a visit from a doctor, a call from my brother—seemed interminable. If I looked calm on the surface, inside I was a nervous wreck. Sometimes when I walked out the door of the hospital I was literally shaking. I was unutterably relieved to get outside into the warm summer air, drive the thirty minutes back to my parents' house, sit on the porch with a glass of wine, and watch the neighbors do their summer things, middle-aged men mowing lawns, kids riding bikes, elderly women slowly walking their little dogs. What a relief to see that it was still all going on.

If my father's decline bruised my heart, my mother's suffering crushed it. I was unprepared to see her so changed. Her legs were hugely swollen; she had nausea and diarrhea; often she was unable to eat or drink by herself. My mom respected the expertise of her health care providers, but she was a bossy, confident person and resented hints about her vulnerability. "That's the culprit!" was her mantra—this medication or that food, there was always a misdiagnosis and she knew best. And though illness and age were beating her, she still insisted on being a mother. "Go to the cafeteria, is that all you're eating?" "You don't have to stay, honey, go home, I know you're tired." "Take my credit card, you and your brother go out to dinner." The worst was the C. *diff*, which weakened her physically and made her feel helpless and ashamed. Because C. *diff* is dangerously infectious for elderly patients, her caretakers had to wear PPE. Their efficiency and grace seemed superhuman to me. They lifted and turned my frail mother like they were folding towels. There were some days I would step out into the hall while this was going on, not to be in their way. But some days I wanted to be there. "What a thing for you to see, Annette," my mother said once. I hoped she could not see the tears staining my cheeks. I pitied her excruciatingly. I knew I must have looked bad when one of the nurses turned around after changing my mother and, raising an eyebrow, said to me, "How're *you* doin'?"

Not every day was a horror movie. We played cards, watched game shows on television, or just talked. For days and days in a row, a song kept running through my mother's head: "September Song," by Kurt Weill and Maxwell Anderson. She'd sing the lines, "When the days dwindle down / To a precious few / September…November…" I Googled a few versions on my iPhone, including one by Willie Nelson and another by Frank Sinatra. But the long version recorded by Walter Huston in 1939 was our favorite, not only because of the way he sang it, but because of the story it tells, about an older person who hasn't time to be courted leisurely any more. I would sit at the edge of her bed and hold up my phone for her to listen. "Oh, that's the best," she'd say. Maybe it was a version she had listened to growing up. Maybe this song was playing in her memory now, stuck there in her mind, because she was feeling the days dwindling, or feared that they were. I didn't want to ask her. My mother and I were not extremely close. I am sure now, looking back, that the nervousness and stabbing alarm I was experiencing was because of some war going on inside of me about losing her. I was not always at ease with my mother. I worried I never pleased her, and there were times that I resented her criticism of my choices in life. But I always admired her strength and individualism, and underneath the occasional tensions and tempers, we loved each other deeply. It was mother–daughter love, complex and indelible.

In the year before she died, when we would talk on the phone, Mom sometimes shared things with me about her childhood. My mother's father, a carpenter and all-around laborer, could be hot-tempered and unpredictable. He spared his two daughters, but sometimes beat the two boys. "I was afraid of my father," my mother told me. I never knew, in all my adult life and growing up, that she had stored up so much anger against my grandfather. When he died, though, her feelings were complicated, as were mine when she died, as children's feelings for their parents always are and must be. How is it we know one another so little? My mother's papa beat the boys and terrified the girls. But he was also the man who built her a bicycle from scraps he found in the junkyard.

And he built their brick-and-mortar house, a home my mother loved and felt strongly connected to her entire life. When it was demolished to build some cheap apartments, she wept, something I rarely saw her do. I, too, have beautiful memories of that house on Francis Court. I used to walk there from school every Friday to have supper with my grandparents. My grandmother, Rose, made me lentil soup or an omelet, and then gave me a dime to buy ice cream at the Creme-o-Freeze on the corner. Their big yard had a home-made swing, rows of tomato plants and patches of basil and oregano, and a small pergola with grape vines, real grapes that one of my uncles would try to make wine from. My grandma was four feet ten inches tall. She had the smallest feet in the world, always neatly encased in tiny black peep-toe wedges.

She was soft and round and safe, and when she held me against her apron, she smelled like oregano and bath soap. One of her names for me was "Precious."

When I drove out to the hospital in the morning to sit with my mother, I kept the radio tuned to a noncommercial station my parents liked to listen to that played music from their era—"The Best Music Ever Written" was the station's modest slogan. One sunny morning the DJ was playing songs about love, including one I remembered listening to with my father, Jo Stafford singing "I Love You." Just as I was pulling into the hospital parking lot, the DJ started to share a personal anecdote. His grandson had come home from school and told him that they were learning about needs and wants. Needs were air and food. Wants were toys and vacations. "What about love," the teacher asked her class. "Is love a need or a want?" The grandson answered confidently that love was a need, but the teacher corrected him. The DJ—I could almost see him scratching his head—said slowly, "Well, I didn't understand that. I don't understand that answer. So I told my grandson that I didn't know if I agreed with the teacher. I thought *he* was right. Love is a need. Or I always thought so." I sat in the parking lot for a few minutes, wondering how a teacher could tell a child that love was only a want. Did she get this from some scientific study? Didn't anyone ever give her a stuffed animal, I thought? How could a caretaker of *children* tell them such thing?

I got off the elevator, went to my mother's room, settled down as usual, and told her that I had been sitting in the parking lot listening to the radio. I told her the DJ's story. "What do you think?" I asked. "Oh *noooo*," she said, in that absolute way she had (my mother was very sure of her opinions, always). "Uh-uh. Love is a need. That teacher's wrong." She looked down at her hands, shaking her head. "Love is a need," she murmured. "Love is a need."

Oliver Twist ends with Oliver and Rose looking at a stone memorial to Oliver's mother, Rose's sister, that has been placed in the wall of a village chapel:

> Within the altar of the old village church there stands a white marble tablet, which bears as yet but one word: "AGNES." There is no coffin in that tomb; and may it be many, many years, before another name is placed above it! But, if the spirits of the Dead ever come back to earth, to visit spots hallowed by the love—the love beyond the grave—of those whom they knew in life, I believe that the shade of Agnes sometimes hovers round that solemn nook. I believe it none the less because that nook is in a Church, and she was weak and erring. (53)

In writing the ending of *Oliver Twist*, Dickens may have been thinking of his beloved young sister-in-law, Mary Hogarth, who died in Dickens's arms at the age of 17, on May 7, 1837. Because of Dickens's bereavement, there was no June 1837 number of *Oliver Twist*. Dickens thought Mary a paragon of womanly purity and virtue. He dreamt about her for months afterward, and expressed a wish to be buried next to her. (Her grave is in Kensal Green Cemetery. I literally stumbled on it during a walk there in the 1990s.) Dickens's grief at Mary's death surely mitigates the barbarity and terror of the world of *Oliver Twist*. He will not believe that a child as good and pure as he believed Mary to be would have no gentle influence on those who survive her. And this is Dickens's elemental belief at the end of *Oliver Twist*: love, even after death, hallows us.

At the end of Carol Reed's *Oliver!* Fagin and the Dodger meet up once again and decide to form a partnership. As the sun rises on the new day, they link arms and dance upon the cobblestones, singing a reprise of Fagin's theme song, "Reviewing the Situation." It is a marvelous, funny ending, and my father and I loved it. But as we watch them skipping down a lane of shuttered shops, the camera swiftly moves to follow a carriage into a leafy London square, and gradually the jaunty last chords of "I'm Reviewing the Situation" blur and become overpowered by Oliver's theme, "Where Is Love?" Oliver gets out of the carriage and runs to Mrs. Bedwin (Megs Jenkins) who is waiting on the steps of his new home. She holds him cherishingly in her arms. The film ends with a close-up of Oliver's face against her apron, as "Where Is Love?" gently swells and resolves. The expression of relief on the boy's face seems absolutely real. Mark Lester is not acting any more. He is home, he is safe, the ordeal of making this film and of being Oliver Twist is over.

I seemed to have forgotten that *Oliver!* does not end with Fagin and the Dodger skipping into the future. But of course, it couldn't end that way, if Reed wanted to respect Lionel Bart's intentions. *Oliver!* ends in the sunny London square, with Oliver and Mrs. Bedwin. Mrs. Bedwin is a minor character, only a servant. She is mentioned by name only once in Vernon Harris's screenplay, and she barely has any lines. Her longest scene is before the "Who Will Buy?" extravaganza, when she opens the curtains of Oliver's room and lets the morning stream in.

In Dickens's novel, Oliver is very fond of Mrs. Bedwin. He likes listening to her, he trusts her. Mrs. Bedwin knows children. She knows them better than the doctor who thinks Oliver is hungry when he isn't, and thinks he is not thirsty when he is. When Oliver allegedly absconds with Mr. Brownlow's books and a five pound note, Mrs. Bedwin defends him unhesitatingly. "He was a dear, grateful, gentle child, sir," she tells old Grimwig indignantly. "I know what children are, sir; and have done these forty years; and people who can't say the same, shouldn't say anything about them." (42) She has faith in Oliver. She *knows* he could not have done what he is being accused of. When Oliver begins to recover from his illness, his nearest companion is always Mrs. Bedwin. She tells him stories about her "amiable and handsome daughter" who is married and lives in the country, and about her son, a merchant in the West Indies, who writes letters to her four times a year. (14) (Although in Chapter 41, she refers to "my own dear children, dead and gone since I was a lightsome young creature.") When Oliver is returned to Mr. Brownlow, he "sprang into her arms" and the two of them go off "to compare notes at leisure." (41) She straightens Oliver's collars, combs his long hair, tucks him into bed. She even teaches him to play cribbage. They keep each other company. And they like to talk: "One evening…as he was sitting talking to Mrs. Bedwin…" (14)

Three days after Oliver has been brought to Mr. Brownlow's, when he is still too weak to walk, Mrs. Bedwin has him carried downstairs into "the little housekeeper's room, which belonged to her." She sets him up by the fire-side and takes a comfortable seat beside him:

> "You're very, very kind to me, ma'am," said Oliver.
> "Well, never you mind that, my dear," said the old lady; "that's got nothing to do with your broth; and it's full time you had it; for the doctor says Mr. Brownlow may come in to see you this morning; and we must get up our best looks, because the better we look, the more he'll be pleased." And with this, the old lady applied herself to warming up, in a little saucepan, a basin full of broth: strong enough, Oliver thought, to furnish an ample dinner when reduced

to the regulation strength, for three hundred and fifty paupers, at the lowest computation. (12)

And so Oliver eats the nice broth Mrs. Bedwin has prepared for him—delicious broth, with bits of salted, toasted bread broken into it. Mrs. Bedwin strokes his hair, tells him things, they laugh together. And she feeds Oliver, tea sometimes, or wine-and-water and toast. She gives him the beautiful strong broth. And Oliver embraces her and blesses her. As if he would never want anything more.

> I wish my parents had been musicians
> and left me themselves transformed into sound,
> or that I could believe in the stars
> as the radiant bodies of the dead.
> Then I could stand in the dark, pointing out
> my mother and father to all
> who did not know them, how they shimmer,
> how they keep getting brighter
> as we keep moving toward each other.[33]

2

BLESSED LITTLE ROOM

Acouple of years ago, when I offered a seminar on Charles Dickens at my university, only three students signed up, so the course was canceled. Some of my colleagues were politely incredulous. Or maybe they were pretending. Perhaps they had forgotten what it was like to read Dickens. Remember "Lord Coodle, and Sir Thomas Doodle, and the Duke of Foodle, and all the fine gentlemen in office, down to Zoodle," and how tiresome that got after the fourth or fifth time around?[1] The people who asked me how only three students could have signed up for Charles Dickens probably did not remember what an endurance test Dickens can be for a lot of readers—and how much more for Generation Z.

But a year or so later for some reason, in the spring of 2020, I still wanted to read Dickens. I proposed another course, this time addressed to the attention spans of the young (now, perhaps, the attention spans of us all). I called it Slow Dickens. In fourteen weeks, we would read just three novels. I thought that by slowing Dickens way down—de-accelerating to something like 2,000 pages instead of the usual 5,000—my students would have a better shot at appreciating him. This *wouldn't* be an endurance test. We'd enjoy Dickens, and we'd also learn how to read complex works of literature closely and carefully.

Due to the scheduling genius of my department head, there was only one author seminar I was competing with this time—and Dickens *had* to have the edge over William Faulkner. My class filled with 15 upper-class English majors. I built in lots of presentations and short papers where students could perform targeted close readings. At our leisurely pace, I thought we could look at the constraints of serialization, Dickens's innovations in Victorian publishing, and even examine the illustrations to his novels. We would pore over Dickens's style and use of symbolic patterns, his emerging social criticism, the peculiarities of his characterization, and the indelible portrait of his city, Victorian London. I wanted to study Dickens surgically, the way my fortunate colleagues with fewer pages to cover in a semester teach their students to read a scene in *Othello*, or lead them through a poem by Donne. It was Dickens frame-by-frame, I thought. Slow Dickens! I would make it impossible for students to dismiss Dickens as too old, too boring, too sappy, too long (on the first day, one student even threw me the bone that Dickens got paid by the word). This was going to be a class about how to read a writer central to Western culture with real attention. This was going to be a class about reading patiently and pointedly, about narrow, close, appreciative reading.

Almost right away something was off. I felt ill at ease. Starting with *Oliver Twist*, one of my favorites, a novel close to my heart and one I've taught many times, I was having trouble talking about Dickens to undergraduates. Baffled and depressed, I confessed to some of my colleagues, "I have nothing to say about *Oliver Twist*. I can't think of anything to say to them." Yes, I was declaring things about Newgate novels and the Poor Law, and we examined some of Cruikshank's illustrations. But I felt I was putting on an act.

Dickens's bursting imagination, his wildly original language, his whole vivid world felt more uncanny than ever. Dickens was *so good*—quite beautiful, and quite terrifying. In my class, I was ventriloquizing someone who had studied Dickens and knew his work, but now I felt I did not know him at all. What felt worse was that the wondering absorption inherent in the act of reading Dickens—the imaginative surrender, the delight—seemed to be elsewhere. All this verbalizing and explaining was getting in the way. I just wanted to read his novels and have my own experience with them. Dickens was asking me to enter completely into his imaginative world, but that loving, urgent invitation kept getting pushed out by some critical agenda. Where had Dickens gone, I wondered. How did the enchantment and fun and mystery get squeezed out of him?

Then on March 11 my university announced that students would not return to campus after spring break because of Covid-19. I was halfway through the course, almost finished with *Dombey and Son*, just eight chapters from shore. But when we finally got back to our new virtual class after two weeks without any contact, *Dombey* felt far, far away. We had to get going with *David Copperfield*: four monthly parts each week, with the last double number in week five, and week six reserved for secondary sources and any necessary catching up. This was slower than I'd planned, but there was no reason we couldn't continue the discussion remotely and non-synchronously. It might even be fun: 16 people, all in different cities, reading *David Copperfield* together. I told the class we were telepathically linked across time and space through Charles Dickens. Maybe Dickens would become an inner resource—students would escape from family life and the stress of the new normal by retreating into their bedrooms to read *David*

Copperfield, just as David reads the eighteenth-century novels that belonged to his father in the little room at the top of Blunderstone Rookery, what David calls "that blessed little room," "as if for life."[2]

I won't detail the progress of this remote class. I carried on with it "as if"—*as if* all 15 students were in their rooms reading the monthly numbers of *David Copperfield* for life, *as if* they were checking out all the mini-lectures, articles, and PowerPoints I posted for them, *as if* they weren't stressed about graduation, the job market, their family, their friends, *as if* this would be over soon and we would go back to something like normal education, normal life.

I tried to maintain a sense of community remotely, but it was like waving from shore at a ship moving ever closer to the horizon line. Ahoy! Awast! (as Captain Cuttle would say). What do you think of Steerforth? Should David marry Dora? But strangely, after a while, and without intending it, I stopped worrying about teaching the novel. I was just reading *David Copperfield*. My leather chair in the study was a comfortable sanctuary ("that blessed little room"). The unusual quiet on my street, the absence of traffic noise and student commotion—the fraternity guys on the corner had vacated the premises—added to the feeling of being on a springtime retreat. Not a skateboard humming down the hill, not a scooter scraping the road. Just a few birds and the eternally yapping terriers, Rocky and Rascal, who live two houses down. Bulletins about the pandemic throbbed in the distance. Yet I have never before read a novel by Dickens in such an oddly tranquil way.

George Orwell wrote in 1940 that much of Dickens was "bad and silly."[3] Yet there is genuine lyricism in Dickens. One passage in *David Copperfield* stood out to me that spring. It occurs at the beginning of Chapter 52, when David is in Canterbury in obedience to Mr. Micawber's mysterious summons. David, Aunt Betsey, Traddles, and Mr. Dick have said goodbye to Dora, who insisted she would do very well without them. David is hanging around the city just after dawn, killing time before his appointment:

> Early in the morning, I sauntered through the dear old tranquil streets, and again mingled with the shadows of the venerable gateways and churches. The rooks were sailing about the cathedral towers; and the towers themselves, overlooking many a long unaltered mile of the rich country and its pleasant streams, were cutting the bright morning air, as if there were no such thing as change on earth. Yet the bells, when they sounded, told me sorrowfully of change in everything; told me of their own age, and my pretty Dora's youth; and of the many, never old, who had lived and loved and died, while the reverberations of the bells had hummed through the rusty armour of the Black Prince hanging up within, and, motes upon the deep of Time, had lost themselves in air, as circles do in water. (52)

The cathedral towers, the bright morning air, the rooks sailing the heavens—these beautiful things, always there, evince continuity, "as if there were no such thing as change on earth." But the humming church-bells, their reverberations lingering through centuries, haunt David. All things change, and he is coming to know it, as we all must come to know it. Yet for all his setbacks and griefs, David manages to summon a mood of calm inevitability, of acceptance and forbearance. Maybe it was the tenderness of *David Copperfield* I needed that Covid spring. An older world, and an older person looking back, telling me that worries can dissolve like circles on water. That Time will take care of things.

In Chapter 4, young David is learning to cope with the cruel changes that have taken place in his home after his mother remarries, and the Murdstone "firmness" is the law. He describes shutting himself up in that room at the top of the house with his father's old books:

> The natural result of this treatment, continued, I suppose, for some six months or more, was to make me sullen, dull, and dogged. I was not made the less so by my sense of being daily more and more shut out and alienated from my mother. I believe I should have been almost stupefied but for one circumstance.
>
> It was this. My father had left a small collection of books in a little room upstairs, to which I had access (for it adjoined my own) and which nobody else in our house ever troubled. From that blessed little room, Roderick Random, Peregrine Pickle, Humphrey Clinker, Tom Jones, the Vicar of Wakefield, Don Quixote, Gil Blas, and Robinson Crusoe, came out, a glorious host, to keep me company. They kept alive my fancy, and my hope of something beyond that place and time,—they, and the Arabian Nights, and the Tales of the Genii,—and did me no harm; for whatever harm was in some of them was not there for me; I knew nothing of it. It is astonishing to me now, how I found time, in the midst of my porings and blunderings over heavier themes, to read those books as I did. It is curious to me how I could ever have consoled myself under my small troubles (which were great troubles to me), by impersonating my favourite characters in them—as I did—and by putting Mr. and Miss Murdstone into all the bad ones—which I did too. I have been Tom Jones (a child's Tom Jones, a harmless creature) for a week together. I have sustained my own idea of Roderick Random for a month at a stretch, I verily believe. I had a greedy relish for a few volumes of Voyages and Travels—I forget what, now—that were on those shelves; and for days and days I can remember to have gone about my region of our house, armed with the centre-piece out of an old set of boot-trees—the perfect realization of Captain Somebody, of the Royal British Navy, in danger of being beset by savages, and resolved to sell his life at a great price. The Captain never lost dignity, from having his ears boxed with the Latin Grammar. I did; but the Captain was a Captain and a hero, in despite of all the grammars of all the languages in the world, dead or alive.

This was my only and my constant comfort. When I think of it, the picture always rises in my mind, of a summer evening, the boys at play in the churchyard, and I sitting on my bed, reading as if for life. (4)

Phenomenological theories of reading recognize this capacity to release the self into the imagined world of books. Wolfgang Iser describes how great literature "transforms reading into a creative process that is far above mere perception of what is written. The literary text activates our own faculties, enabling us to recreate the world it presents."[4] Reading is a process of continual modification as we read, a movement back and forth between the inner reading world and the outside real one. In *The Poetics of Space*, Gaston Bachelard writes, "the joy of reading seems to be a reflection of the joy of writing, as though the reader were the writer's ghost." The reader "participates in the joy of creation."[5] Virginia Woolf, who was not particularly fond of Dickens, said something similar about Dickens's characters in her essay on *David Copperfield*, from 1925. "This is the power which cannot fade or fail in its effect—the power not to analyse or to interpret, but to produce…characters who exist not in detail, not accurately or exactly, but abundantly in a cluster of wild and yet extraordinarily revealing remarks, bubble climbing on the top of bubble as the breath of the creator fills them. And the fecundity and apparent irreflectiveness have a strange effect. They make *creators* of us and not merely readers and spectators."[6]

It is not just reading that consoles David; he doesn't read to escape or disappear. He joyfully *creates* the tale along with the author. He is awakened to possibilities he would not have imagined without the opening these fictions offered him. The plots and characters seep into his world and inhabit it, just as Dickens's own early reading had. "Every barn in the neighbourhood, every stone in the church, and every foot of the churchyard, had some association of its own, in my mind, connected with these books, and stood for some locality made famous in them," David says. "I have seen Tom Pipes go climbing up the church-steeple; I have watched Strap, with the knapsack on his back, stopping to rest himself upon the wicket-gate; and I know that Commodore Trunnion held that club with Mr. Pickle, in the parlour of our little village alehouse." (4) He discovers, remarkably, that his real world is enriched and intensified by the imagined one, that they almost overlap.

For David, *Peregrine Pickle* or *Robinson Crusoe* feed a desperate optimism. The books "kept alive my fancy, and my hope of something beyond that place and time." Reading gives him space to dream about a different kind of reality. And the old books are a precious refuge. When he returns home from school for the long holiday, his only escape from the Murdstones' icy law is "to keep myself as much out of their way as I could; and many a wintry hour did I hear the church clock strike, when I was sitting in my cheerless bedroom, wrapped in my little great-coat, poring over a book." (8) Reading also helps David mentally revise his experiences of cruelty and injustice. He gains control over his life "by impersonating my favourite characters . . . and by putting Mr. and Miss Murdstone into all the bad ones." Because he reads innocently, without the moral uptightness of the censoring adult, nothing he reads can harm him. Utterly powerless, he finds ways to circumvent humiliation and punishment through the larger-than-life heroes in his stories of adventure. Mr. Murdstone might whip him for not knowing his lessons, but he has a private defense in the thought of the Captain who never lost his dignity, who remained "a Captain and a hero." Young David uses books as tools for psychic growth, even for survival. And of course, he becomes a writer of stories himself.

David is not a studious, critical reader. He is neither suspicious nor resisting, he does not perform close readings, he is not even inquisitive. But he is a true and dedicated reader nonetheless— maybe he is Dickens's ideal reader. "To read a novel is a difficult and complex art," writes Woolf. "You must be capable not only of great fineness of perception, but of great boldness of imagination if you are going to make use of all that the novelist—the great artist—gives you."[7] Reading a novel requires immense mental labor. Yet, paradoxically, to read well you also have to be relaxed, in a state of what Bachelard calls "psychic détente."[8] "It is astonishing to me now, how I found time, in the midst of my porings and blunderings over heavier themes," David says, "to read those books as I did." But it makes perfect sense. For unlike his lessons, *Peregrine Pickle* and *Don Quixote* don't weigh on David, it's not material he's going to be tested on. These books lighten the burden of his harrowing young life. Reading in that space of mental liberty, his child's consciousness begins to develop, a self is being staged. David carries those stories in his mind for weeks and months at a time. They remain "psychologically alive" for him over many years.[9] He is, truly, never finished reading them.

In my Slow Dickens seminar, I wanted my students to read deliberately, and I had the right motive—to teach a patient analysis of the details in Dickens's fiction. But surgical close reading is not necessarily what makes someone a good reader, and especially, perhaps, not a good reader of Dickens—instinctively a phenomenologist if anyone was. Mastery of the text and a pile of facts is not always what people need, young people especially. In one of his "Talks to Teachers," William James suggested that if the teacher appeals to a student's "passive attention," the lesson goes much more pleasantly. The student can pay attention to the *feelings* a book arouses, and in that way discover for herself what is important, instead of boxing it up into contexts and conceptualizations. In her book on the transactional theory of reading, *The Reader, The Text, the Poem*, Louise Rosenblatt writes that what happens "between the reader and what he senses the words as pointing to" is a paradox, for the reader is required to "call forth from memory of his world what the visual or auditory stimuli symbolize for him, yet he feels the ensuing work as part of the world outside himself."[10] Literature points inward, toward private networks of memories, images, and symbols, and also outward, toward a world richly populated by other consciousnesses and other stories.

Bachelard asks why a great novel of reverie—and *David Copperfield* surely is one—has to become a novel of historical and social facts, must "become bogged down in the objections of the critical spirit or become enmeshed in repression."[11] Sometimes we have to read with what Marion Milner has called "wide attention," a "second way of perceiving," without determined purposefulness.[12] Reading this way that Covid spring, I noticed new things about Dickens as a writer, his world seemed brighter in my mind's eye. I could see his sunrises and sunsets, his love of changing urban skies. I noticed his minute attention to what characters' hands and eyes are doing. And I noted again what I call Dickens's throwaways, the strange, superfluous details that he can't resist—as when Miss Murdstone presents Dora with her "uncongenial cheek, the little wrinkles in it filled with hair powder." (26)

Reading with wide attention is taking notice of what you notice—the key word is still *attention*, but without the prosecutorial connotations. The mind catches in its net whatever thoughts or images happen to float in, there is no strict analytical agenda. This is creative reading, and it is how young David reads. The outside world never vanishes, but his imagination augments that reality, he obtains a sense of calm in spite of the disturbances of the world. He is on the edge of reality and fantasy, and that is an exciting place to be. Davey reads with ardor and absorption, but his attention is ungrasping, he doesn't need to know everything about the book in his hands. Reading this way becomes for David a type of apprenticeship for life. And especially, perhaps, an apprenticeship for love.

When I was a graduate student and then a young teacher, the higher ups in academia usually justified the study of literature as practice in critical thinking inflected with political activism. Rarely did anyone talk about pleasure, let alone about love. I had been teaching for almost twenty years before I found a mentor who used that word earnestly and without embarrassment, not only about reading but about teaching. I still cannot trace the genesis of my acquaintance with Marshall Gregory's work. I was sitting in my office one day, literally staring out the window, when I seemed to receive a message from the Beyond: *Google him*. So I did, and then invited him to come to campus in February 2008 to give a talk about reading and ethics. I had never met him before, but we clicked, just like that. What an important person Greg was in my personal and professional life, so generous, gentle, and open. I knew him for barely five years before pancreatic cancer got him at the age of 72. We had only met in person twice. The first was the time he came to my university to give his lecture, the second just two months before he died when I made a trip to Indianapolis to say goodbye. He died on December 30, 2012. I was in Boston at the MLA Convention, of all places, when his daughter called to tell me.

Before he died, Greg had been writing a book about teaching, and in September 2013 his publisher sent me the manuscript to blurb. "What's Love Got to Do With It?" is the title of my favorite chapter. It begins, "Perhaps the most difficult dynamic to see clearly in any classroom is the pulsing of love," for Greg held the controversial conviction that "teaching will not work without love." He said he knew this was true early in his career, "from some deep source inside, although it has taken me a long time to work out the actual view that my intuition was rooted in." This chapter was his careful, sophisticated analysis of that basic intuition, a personal and philosophical meditation on the kind of love a teacher should have for his students. He pointed out that pride and vanity will get in the way of love (academic pride being a particularly ugly variety), but if teachers can concentrate on *agape*, we will see our students as human beings who are embarked on their own unique journeys, and we will teach them effectively, so they can discover their own secrets in the books we assign, and learn something about who they are.[13]

Good teachers are few and far between in Dickens's novels. The nice ones, like Mr. Pocket in *Great Expectations* or Mr. Mell and Mr. Strong in *David Copperfield*, are scatter-brained and ineffectual, and the mean ones are positively sadistic—Wackford Squeers in *Nicholas Nickleby* is the prototype. Other teachers are well-meaning and clueless, like Mr. McChoakumchild in *Hard Times* or Dr. Blimber in *Dombey and Son*, wedded to a system of facts, forcing, and cramming, as if children were hothouse plants or little empty pitchers to be filled up with information.

> They knew no rest from the pursuit of stony-hearted verbs, savage noun-substantives, inflexible syntactic passages, and ghosts of exercises that appeared to them in their dreams. Under the forcing system, a young gentleman usually took leave of his spirits in three weeks.... [And] at the end of the first twelvemonth had arrived at the conclusion, from which he never afterwards departed, that all the fancies of the poets, and lessons of the sages, were a mere collection of words and grammar, and had no other meaning in the world.[14]

The tendency to reduce poetry and literature to mere fragments of grammar hopefully has had its day. In any case, there is not much *agape* at Creakle's establishment. David never mentions a single book he read at either Creakle's or Dr. Strong's. But the novels that belonged to his father are permanently etched in his memory. There are so many examples to prove this. When he is a proctor and has returned to Yarmouth for Barkis's funeral, Davey does not just say "I left Peggotty and Mr. Peggotty at the gate." He writes, "I parted from them at the wicket-gate, where visionary Strap had rested with Roderick Random's knapsack in the days of yore." (31) On the first Sunday after Mr. Micawber is imprisoned, David remembers with a thrill of terror "when Roderick Random was in a debtors' prison, there was a man there with nothing on him but an old rug." (11) When Mr. Barkis takes him away from home to go to school, David says, "Having by this time cried as much as I possibly could, I began to think it was of no use crying any more, especially as neither Roderick Random, nor that Captain in the Royal British Navy, had ever cried, that I could remember, in trying situations." (5) When, amazed, he sees London looming in the distance, he believes "all the adventures of all my favourite heroes to be constantly enacting and re-enacting there." (5) *Robinson Crusoe* supplies David with an image for his feeling of abandonment when he's stranded alone at the booking-office, and feels "More solitary than Robinson Crusoe, who had nobody to look at him and see that he was solitary," and for the feeling of snug aloneness when he gets his own top-floor chambers in Buckingham Street: "It was a wonderfully fine thing to have that lofty castle to myself, and to feel, when I shut my outer door, like Robinson Crusoe, when he had got into his fortification, and pulled his ladder up after him." (5, 24) Reading is *sense-making*. David's stories have shaped his whole way of seeing the world, even late into the novel.

Peggotty's Crocodile Book was Davey's first book, and it has special importance in his development. He always links it to the happy times he spent with Peggotty and his mother in the little parlor. In his attic room at Peggotty's house, the Crocodile Book has its privileged place on a shelf by the head of his bed. Whenever he visits that room and is "turning over the leaves of the crocodile-book (which was always there, upon a little table)" feelings of intense gratitude to Peggotty and Aunt Betsey rise to the surface. (22) Reading is *attachment*. Later, David recalls finding Foxe's Book of Martyrs in an old desk in Peggotty's house. "This precious volume, of which I do not recollect one word," he says, "I immediately discovered and immediately applied myself to; and I never visited the house afterwards, but I kneeled on a chair, opened the casket where this gem was enshrined, spread my arms over the desk, and fell to devouring the book afresh. I was chiefly edified, I am afraid, by the pictures, which were numerous, and represented all kinds of dismal horrors; but the Martyrs and Peggotty's house have been inseparable in my mind ever since, and are now." (10) David doesn't recall a word from The Book of Martyrs. At that time in his life, the words were not what was important. What mattered was that the book was always in the same place every time he went to Peggotty's house. What anchors David's memory is kneeling on a chair, opening the desk, spreading his arms, devouring the pictures. Reading is *ritualistic*. And this episode with The Book of Martyrs comes in his narrative very soon after his mother's death. Perhaps the Book of Martyrs is a ritual compensation for what David has lost, or for something he has to pass through? Or perhaps its horrible pictures externalize young Davey's acute suffering, image forth his own martyrdom? Either way, he puts the object to use and when he no longer needs the book psychologically, the intensity of his response to the pictures dims. As a young man, when he and Steerforth pay a visit to Peggotty and Barkis, David says, "We made merry in the little parlour, where the Book of Martyrs, unthumbed since my time, was laid out upon the desk as of old, and where I now turned over its terrific pictures, remembering the old sensations they had awakened, but not feeling them." (21) The Book of Martyrs, like the Crocodile Book (which Peggotty has in her pocket in the very last chapter of *David Copperfield*), can be stored in the past. David has new books to read and to write, new stories to tell and to make his own.

In an illustration by Harry Furniss for a 1910 edition of *David Copperfield*, David the famous author sits at his desk dreaming of his characters (Figure 2.1).[15] The idea for this trope was borrowed from Robert W. Buss's famous unfinished painting, *Dickens's Dream* (there were also several English and American illustrators who played on the theme of "Dickens Among His Characters"

Figure 2.1 Harry Furniss's illustration for Volume 10 of the Charles Dickens Library Edition of *David Copperfield* (1910), facing the title-page.

in obituary tributes after Dickens's death in 1870). Furniss's drawing inadvertently reveals something essential about David's psychology. As he sits at his writing desk, David does not conjure up Robinson Crusoe or Peregrine Pickle as he did as a child. Nor is he dreaming up characters for his own fictions (whatever those may be). David is dreaming of the people in his own life—Micawber, Mr. Dick, Peggotty, Aunt Betsey, Steerforth, Dora, Agnes, they are all easily identifiable. He dreams his life as if it were a marvelous story, where other people have their parts to play, swirling around the central plot of his own journey. David possesses what James describes as the "unsharable feeling that each one of us has of the pinch of his individual destiny as he privately feels it rolling out on fortune's wheel."[16] It makes your life seem meaningful and special when you choose to see it this way.

David begins his nightly storytelling at Salem House after he idly observes to Steerforth "that something or somebody—I forget what now—was like something or somebody in Peregrine Pickle." (7) Why does David say this? Does he subconsciously want to be the author of these stories? Does he need therapeutically to repeat them? Because he has the books by heart, he can tell them every night, ceremonially, like Scheherazade—again, as if for life. Looking back, David says, "Whatever I had within me that was romantic and dreamy, was encouraged by so much storytelling in the dark; and in that respect the pursuit may not have been very profitable to me. But the being cherished as a kind of plaything in my room, and the consciousness that this accomplishment of mine was bruited about among the boys, and attracted a good deal of notice to me though I was the youngest there, stimulated me to exertion." (7) David is honest about his need for acceptance. He's a budding author, after all, craving self expression, authority, approval, he is someone who enjoys getting people emotionally involved, amusing them, manipulating them. Reading is power, it is *validating*. It is a huge emotional deprivation when the group storytelling is taken away—we know this because when David is destitute, he decides to sleep in a haystack outside the walls of Salem House, where he imagines "it would be a kind of company to have the boys, and the bed-room where I used to tell the stories, so near me." (13) He even attempts to entertain some workers at Murdstone & Grinby's with "the old readings; which were fast perishing out of my remembrance." David tells us that the carman, Tipp, and the foreman, Gregory, call him respectfully by his given name *only* during those periods of reading, "when we were very confidential." (11) Reading is also *intimacy*. He and Agnes shared a love of reading as children (Dora screams when David tries to read Shakespeare to her). After his three-year sojourn in Europe, when he returns to Canterbury, he notes that the "books that Agnes and I had read together, were on their shelves; and the desk where I had laboured at my lessons, many a night, stood yet at the same old corner of the table." (60) That's another thing David likes about reading, its furniture and accessories, shelves, tables, desks, boxes, bureaus, the whole glorious apparatus of storing, arranging, and rediscovering books.

For David, reading is *security*, as in Barthes: "The pleasure of the text can be defined by praxis (without any danger of repression): the time and place of reading: house, countryside, near mealtime, the lamp, family where it should be, i.e., close but not too close...Extraordinary ego-reinforcement (by fantasy), the unconscious muffled."[17] Not having to repress the pleasure, getting ego-reinforcement without having to worry about taking on a project of self-improvement, these are key requirements for young David, for me, for any reader. I will not be the first person to notice that as a child reading is object-relational for him, a space of *play*, perhaps a symbol of maternal union. He faintly remembers learning the alphabet at his mother's knee.

> To this day, when I look upon the fat black letters in the primer, the puzzling novelty of their shapes, and the easy good-nature of O and Q and S, seem to present themselves again before me as they used to do. But they recall no feeling of disgust or reluctance. On the contrary, I seem to have walked along a path of flowers as far as the crocodile-book, and to have been cheered by the gentleness of my mother's voice and manner all the way. (4)

When his lessons become laborious and intimidating, when Murdstone's in charge, when mother is silenced or removed, Davey's emotions are stifled, his whimsy clamped down. He becomes "sullen, dull, and dogged." Angry enough to bite. Where does a child put those feelings? What is he supposed to do with them? So David makes the Murdstones the bad guys in his re-imagined stories. Reading is *projection*. An escape valve.

Nine months into pandemic lockdown, in mid-December 2020, my partner, Charles, who has never read a novel by Dickens in his life, nor any Victorian novel ever, wanted to read *A Christmas Carol* aloud to me, incrementally, one Stave a night. This was out of character. This was unusual. To be very clear, this is not something we do every Christmas, or at all, because to be very honest, Charles is not a reader of fiction. This idea was a Covid-19 special, a way to bring a spirit of hope to the season. Maybe he thought of it as something to do together (even though for the past ten months we had been almost constantly together). Whatever the reason or the motive, I was charmed. And so one evening after dinner, we commenced.

On the long drives to visit our families in Indiana and Ohio at Christmas, we sometimes listened to different audio books of *A Christmas Carol*, trying to "get in the spirit" on the unlovely, slush-smattered Pennsylvania Turnpike. But this nightly reading aloud at home is entirely different. It gets at something quite primitive. Charles has wonderful vocal stamina, intuitively great pacing (he is a musician), and an evenly modulated voice which is unthe-atrical while being perfectly attune to what's going on dramatically. Easier to see the book on his iPhone, so no bright lights, we're in semi-darkness like David and the boys at Salem House. Blankets and lounging clothes. I sit in my leather chair in my blessed room with the dog, Jasper, curled by my side, Charles sits in his chair by the bookcase. When a trusted voice reads a familiar book in a dark room, it kindles such joy, such forgotten childhood pleasures, everything softens into wonder. It took only about an hour to read one Stave, but I lost all sense of time, it felt like the whole evening. Charles's voice, Dickens's words, the fireplace smell, the closed curtains, the breathing dog—what was this long lost emotion, this pure satisfaction? How eager and excited I was to hear a story I have read and taught dozens of times. *A Christmas Carol* felt abso-lutely new, I heard sentences I never registered before, saw pic-tures in my mind that were never there when I read the book silently to myself. Processing language with your eyes and brain requires some concentration, but being an auditor frees you up, you become "'an open force field' into whom sounds are being breathed."[18] I listened, squirmy and delighted, safe and secure, rapt in the moment. When we first started dating, Charles's eight-year-old son sometimes spent the night at my house. Some nights we made up ghost stories in the dark in front of the fire, or played charades, laughing at our silliness. Then we established a nightly reading ritual, where we would all get in bed and trade off reading stories from the Brothers Grimm. Doing this gave me deep, deep pleasure. I remember thinking, *Oh, now I get it it, this is why people want to have children.* That was a little cynical of me. But how nice to bundle together with a book, what a close and loving ritual! Warm bed, dark night, a voice breathing words and weaving pictures. Remember how that used to feel?

Steerforth enjoys hearing young David's stories at night, they entertain him. But they never take over his imagination, never find a root there—not that we're told. This is a fundamental difference between David and Steerforth. When he is stopping in London on his way to Yarmouth, in Chapter 19, David goes to Covent Garden Theater. He is willingly mesmerized, completely taken in:

> Being then in a pleasant frame of mind…I resolved to go to the play. It was Covent Garden Theatre that I chose; and there, from the back of a center box, I saw Julius Caesar and the new Pantomime. To have all those noble Romans alive before me, and walking in and out for my entertainment, instead of being the stern taskmasters they had been at school, was a most novel and delightful effect. But the mingled reality and mystery of the whole show, the influence upon me of the poetry, the lights, the music, the company, the smooth stupendous changes of glittering and brilliant scenery, were so dazzling, and opened up such illimitable regions of delight, that when I came out into the rainy street, at twelve o'clock at night, I felt as if I had come from the clouds, where I had been leading a romantic life for ages, to a bawling, splashing, link-lighted, umbrella-struggling, hackney-coach-jostling, patten-clinking, muddy, miserable world. (19)

David is so open to enchantment! On his walk back to his inn, still in the clouds, he feels "a stranger upon earth" until the hustling crowds wake him up. But he luxuriates in the dream again, "revolving the glorious vision all the way," and when he has had his oysters and porter and is sitting in the coffee-room by the fire, he "was so filled with the play, and with the past—for it was, in a manner, like a shining transparency, through which I saw my earlier life moving along—that I don't know when the figure of a handsome well-formed young man dressed with a tasteful easy negligence which I have reason to remember very well, became a real presence to me." The young man is, of course, James Steerforth, who has, coincidentally, also been to Covent Garden Theatre. "What a delightful and magnificent entertainment, Steerforth!" exclaims David. Steerforth laughs at him. "My dear young David, you are a very Daisy.... The daisy of the field, at sunrise, is not fresher than you are. I have been at Covent Garden, too, and there never was a more miserable business." (19)

Steerforth sees stories and plays as a way to get through a dull evening, as mere entertainment. He's too cool, too blasé to be taken in by them, he's basically a consumer. But David—Daisy—sees them as *a shining transparency, through which I saw my earlier life moving along*. The play holds a secret, personal message for David. It tells his own story, refracted with potential meaning for him. Maybe Steerforth is careless about life because whatever he chooses to do at the moment is not necessarily connected to what he does at other moments—that could be a result of his spoiled upbringing, or it could just be how he's wired. I don't want to judge him, philosophers are still debating how the brain processes narratives.[19] And Steerforth is an attractive, complex, and heartbreaking character. But he doesn't see his life in the stories he reads or hears, he doesn't imagine they could be truth-revealing. A lot of people are like that, maybe most people are. Steerforth has a very familiar philosophy:

> "It's a bad job…but the sun sets every day, and people die every minute, and we mustn't be scared by the common lot. If we failed to hold our own, because that equal foot at all men's doors was heard knocking somewhere, every object in this world would slip from us. No! Ride on! Rough-shod if need be, smooth-shod if that will do, but ride on! Ride on over all obstacles, and win the race!" (28)

Intelligent David asks, "And win what race?" "The race that one has started in," Steerforth answers. "Ride on!" David questions, for just a moment, if he should "remonstrate with him upon his desperate way of pursuing any fancy that he took." (28) But he suppresses that thought.

You can see life as a straight line, a race with a prize at the end, or as a story that is unfolding over time, mystery upon mystery, like circles on water. Steerforth's attitude is strong, willful, assertive. It's about winning. David's attitude is more fuzzy, tentative: "*Whether* I shall turn out to be the hero of my own life, or *whether* that station will be held by anybody else, these pages must show." (1) Personally, I am more like David, I like to think of my life as a series of accidental events that I can assemble in a way that makes my life feel meaningful. It is unimportant to me that I am making it up, imposing my own subjective order on random circumstances. Of course I am doing that. It helps me get through the day. As the philosopher Frank Farrell puts it (rather laboriously), "There is perhaps something of evolutionary as well as personal significance in the pleasure we take in the emergence of self-sustaining patterns from what appears scattered and meaningless, [and] in our ability to order a lighter world of representations instead of submitting to the heaviness of things."[20] When he is working at Murdstone and Grinby's and living with the Micawbers, when his life is abject and degraded, his surroundings shabby and disreputable, the adult David, looking back, comprehends how his story-making mind somehow made it tolerable:

> When my thoughts go back, now, to that slow agony of my youth, I wonder how much of the histories I invented for such people hangs like a mist of fancy over well-remembered facts! When I tread the old ground, I do not wonder that I seem to see and pity, going on before me, an innocent romantic boy, making his imaginative world out of such strange experiences and sordid things! (11)

Young David was educated in the school of hard knocks—under the Murdstone regime, at Creakle's school, at Murdstone and Grinby's, with the precarious Micawbers, on the dusty trudge to Dover. His trust was frequently met with abuse, trickery, and indifference by waiters and carters, shopkeepers and tramps, teachers and guardians. Maybe David's early reading did feed his innate dreaminess and naivety, made him more vulnerable, an easy prey. He may have been better off with a little less Smollett and a little more grit. But we cannot know who he would have become, and what he would have done, without the "mist of fancy" that has become such a part of him. It was a gift he preserved and developed, as did Dickens himself, against all the odds.

When she was studying child psychology in the 1920s, Marion Milner recalled "controversies…about whether reading fairy tales and legends was not a waste of time for children, since they would have their work cut out anyway to discover what were the facts about the world, without having the issue confused with fantasy." But she concluded that "it was not only facts about the world that they needed to know, they needed also facts about themselves, and it was only through imaginative symbols of fantasy that they could first express their knowledge of themselves."[21] What David sweetly calls "my strolling fancy" is a means of such self expression. That creative, resilient responsiveness to people and to his environment may have had its root in the solitary hours he spent reading in the upper room at Blunderstone Rookery "as if for life." In that blessed room, long ago, David began to imagine a more various world. He began to dream that there could be something better than what there was. When grown-up David looks back at the days he spent in the little room with his father's books, his feelings of enthusiasm are very easily re-awakened in him. The picture is still vivid: "a summer evening, the boys at play in the churchyard, and I sitting on my bed, reading as if for life." Narrating, adult David knows that human life is full of defeat, betrayal, and loss. He sees the wickedness around him. He has experienced considerable trauma. Yet he can look back with astonishment at everything that has happened to him. Instead of suppressing his childish excitement in those make-believe worlds, he releases it into his writing, as Dickens releases the child within the identifying reader.

David Copperfield is a peculiarly gifted and sensitive boy. Like Dickens, he is a "child of excellent abilities, and with strong powers of observation, quick, eager, delicate, and soon hurt bodily or mentally." (11) An intelligent child with deep feelings and a lively imagination may very naturally find pleasure and solace in storybooks. He might grow into a person for whom writing and literature is a psychological necessity. And so David becomes a famous novelist. But the most important story in David's life, it turns out, is not *Robinson Crusoe* or *Humphrey Clinker*. It is the one his mother told him when he was a child. "Again, and again, and a hundred times again," he says, since the night when he first thinks of running away from London, "I had gone over that old story of my poor mother's about my birth, which it had been one of my great delights in the old time to hear her tell, and which I knew by heart."

> My aunt walked into that story, and walked out of it, a dread and awful personage; but there was one little trait in her behaviour which I liked to dwell on, and which gave me some faint shadow of encouragement. I could not forget how my mother had thought that she felt her touch her pretty hair with no ungentle hand; and though it might have been altogether my mother's fancy, and might have had no foundation whatever in fact, I made a little picture, out of it, of my terrible aunt relenting towards the girlish beauty that I recollected so well and loved so much, which softened the whole narrative. It is very possible that it had been in my mind a long time, and had gradually engendered my determination. (12)

Just as he invented histories for people when he was living with the Micawbers, hanging "like a mist of fancy over well-remembered facts," what sticks with David is his mother's fancy. He notes the one little trait—did it really happen?—that alleviates the narrative, and he acts on the faith of it. David wonders if that story had been in his mind for a long time. Yes, it was always there, stored away until he needed it, just as with all his other stories, because sometimes the need for the story is greater than the need for the fact. David trusts the story.

I read *David Copperfield* again in the winter of 2020, in drear December. I read my same marked-up teaching edition, mostly in the same chair in the same room, almost as slowly as I had read it in March and April, when I was teaching the novel in my Slow Dickens seminar. Was that only last spring? Eight months ago? The blur of time during lockdown created an even stranger déjà vu feeling. When this is over, I thought, will I look back and see myself in that blessed little room eternally reading *David Copperfield*, as spring turns into summer, then fall, then winter, then back to spring? Will I be reading *David Copperfield* forever, *as if* there would again be a world outside of this room, a world of concerts and restaurants, vacations and classrooms?

My small city felt so quiet between March and December. Time passed, but stealthily. Friends and colleagues lost elderly parents who were far away. Charles's mother died on July 1. We drove ten hours from Virginia to Indiana, but we did not make it in time to say goodbye. A dear friend's fiancé died in the hospital in May as they were planning their wedding, another close friend was diagnosed with cancer, relatives in Florida were hospitalized with the virus, and a 53-year-old professor at my university died from Covid in January. These things are always happening, but somehow they seemed to stand out, black strokes on a monotonous calendar. Anniversaries passed, both happy and sad, which I and others marked separately, as we marked the curve of the pandemic and the numbers on the Covid dashboard. Yet with all that was going on, I felt ok. My Zoom poetry classes were the bright spots in each day, I had such affection for those sweet, bewildered students. And I had Dickens to think about. My therapist, Patricia, once characterized me as a "deep introvert," so I wasn't missing out on anything I normally would do. I was happy at home. And compared to so many others, I had a big cushion: a reliable job, a comfortable home, a partner, a university community, no small children to home-school, and no aging parents in long-term care facilities.

In my wintertime reading of *David Copperfield*, I noted again the passage in Chapter 52 that stood out to me when I read the novel in the spring, the scene where David walks the streets of Canterbury in the early morning and hears the reverberations of the bells. This time in my reading, I noticed that David had been here twice before, and that each time he makes an association with a woman in his life. The first time, he passes through the city on his way to find his aunt in Dover, in Chapter 13. He associates a "fanciful picture of my mother in her youth, before I came into the world" with "the sunny street of Canterbury, dozing as it were in the hot light; and with the sight of its old houses and gateways, and the stately, grey Cathedral, with the rooks sailing round the towers." The second time is in Chapter 39, when David stops at Canterbury on his way to see to his aunt's cottage. This is when he is a proctor with Mr. Spenlow, and in the throes of young love. "Strange to say, that quiet influence which was inseparable in my mind from Agnes, seemed to pervade even the city where she dwelt." He notes again the "venerable cathedral towers, and the old jackdaws and rooks whose airy voices made them more retired than perfect silence would have done." The sunny streets and the cathedral, with the rooks sailing around the towers—there were no rooks at Blunderstone Rookery, but here they seem to be miraculously and forever sailing—make him think about the passage of time, and about women: his dead mother, Agnes, and "my pretty Dora's youth." David cannot consciously admit it yet, but he knows what the tolling bells are saying to him. He knows that he and Dora do not have much time left together. She dies in the next chapter.

People don't usually think of *David Copperfield* as a novel about marriage, the way *Middlemarch* is. Yet I found myself troubled and moved by David and Dora's relationship—more than usual, I should say, for the chapters with Dora have always touched me. I never understood Virginia Woolf's comment that Dickens fails "when he has to treat of the mature emotions—the seduction of

Emily, for example, or the death of Dora."[22] The death of Dora? I always thought Dickens treated the death of Dora with economy and restraint, just as he treats David's marriage with honesty and humanity.

There is a long section from Chapter 48 in which David begins to comprehend how hard it is to be an adult and how many compromises he will have to make in his marriage:

> In fulfillment of the compact I have made with myself, to reflect my mind on this paper, I again examine it, closely, and bring its secrets to the light. What I missed, I still regarded—I always regarded—as something that had been a dream of my youthful fancy; that was incapable of realization; that I was now discovering to be so, with some natural pain, as all men did. But that it would have been better for me if my wife could have helped me more, and shared the many thoughts in which I had no partner; and that this might have been; I knew.
>
> Between these two irreconcilable conclusions: the one, that what I felt was general and unavoidable; the other, that it was particular to me, and might have been different: I balanced curiously, with no distinct sense of their opposition to each other. When I thought of the airy dreams of youth that are incapable of realization, I thought of the better state preceding manhood that I had outgrown; and then the contented days with Agnes, in the dear old house, arose before me, like spectres of the dead, that might have some renewal in another world, but never more could be reanimated here.
>
> Sometimes, the speculation came into my thoughts, What might have happened, or what would have happened, if Dora and I had never known each other? But she was so incorporated with my existence, that it was the idlest of all fancies, and would soon rise out of my reach and sight, like gossamer floating in the air.
>
> I always loved her. What I am describing, slumbered, and half awoke, and slept again, in the innermost recesses of my mind. There was no evidence of it in me; I know of no influence it had in anything I said or did. I bore the weight of all our little cares, and all my projects; Dora held the pens; and we both felt that our shares were adjusted as the case required. She was truly fond of me, and

proud of me; and when Agnes wrote a few earnest words in her letters to Dora, of the pride and interest with which my old friends heard of my growing reputation, and read my book as if they heard me speaking its contents, Dora read them out to me with tears of joy in her bright eyes, and said I was a dear old clever, famous boy. (48)

Dickens takes me poignantly and quite bravely to the center of David's inner conflict, to thoughts that must feel familiar to many grown-ups. The dream of my youth is not going to be my life. I must accept this, it happens to everyone sooner or later. I cannot return to the innocent happiness of my childish days, I have outgrown that. But if I had never met Dora, what might have happened? Yet it is wrong to blame her for my stuck feelings. I love her, she is fond and proud of me, and besides, these thoughts come and go, they don't affect how I am with her. These are the wistful secrets of David's heart.

David's reflections remind me a well-known section in Iris Murdoch's essay, "The Idea of Perfection." As I understand it, Murdoch wishes to refute certain ideas in moral philosophy that have been "theorised away," especially "the fact that an unexamined life can be virtuous and the fact that love is a central concept in morals."[23] To make her point, she offers a made-up example. A mother, called M, dislikes her daughter-in-law, called D. The daughter-in-law is "quite a good-hearted girl, but while not exactly common yet certainly unpolished and lacking in dignity and refinement." D also is inclined to be "pert and familiar" and "always tiresomely juvenile." M, however, does not allow her "real opinions of D to appear in any way," and always behaves "correctly" towards her. Time passes (perhaps D has died or emigrated). M could settle down with a fixed image of D and nurse her resentments. Yet, because M is "an intelligent and well-intentioned person, capable of self-criticism, capable of giving careful and just *attention* to an object which confronts her," she examines her opinion of D. And as she thinks more about it, she finds that D is "not vulgar but refreshingly simple, not undignified but spontaneous, not noisy but gay, not tiresomely juvenile but delightfully youthful, and so on." This drama is all happening within her own mind, no one knows about it. "M is engaged in an internal struggle," Murdoch says. "She may for example be tempted to enjoy caricatures of D in her imagination." That could satisfy her disapproving side, and bolster her ego. In real life, it might be hard to say if what M decided about D was right or not—maybe she really is deluding herself about D's merits, and her initial judgment is on the mark. But it is also possible that M is "moved by love and justice," and that she is trying to give D the benefit of the doubt. She is trying to see D "justly and lovingly." This latter view is the one Murdoch prefers.[24]

As harshly as Dickens treated his wife Catherine in after years, as strongly as he identifies with David's disappointments in marriage, as a novelist Dickens understands what a person like Dora might be like from the inside, and he treats her justly. Dora Spenlow, of course, is based on Dickens's first love, Maria Beadnell, when he was her slave at the age of 18. But outside of the revival of certain feelings associated with Maria, Dickens is just very fond of this character. Forster records that "the child-wife Dora…had become a great favourite as he went on."[25] Dickens even named his third daughter, born in the autumn of 1850, Dora Annie (she died eight months later). If we see Dora Spenlow as an airhead, as my worldly-wise students tend to do, that is our (moral) problem. Certainly Dora does not have the wisdom and quiet assurance of

Agnes. But she has innate sweetness of temper, she has lightness of spirit, and with her pagoda for Jip and wanting to hold the pens, she's kind of original. Though people do not treat her rationally—she is totally spoiled, but whose fault is that?—Dora is endearing to almost everyone. She has a "childish, winning way." (37)

It is wrong, as we all know, to advertise impossible fantasies about romantic love to young people and to promise that what they feel at 20 will never change or fade. That's setting them up for failure. Yet, as D. W. Winnicott argues, it's also wrong to do the opposite, and to sell them hard-boiled truths that guarantee their disillusionment. "If one *has been happy*, one can bear distress," Winnicott says.[26] And David and Dora *had been* happy. Yes, I know, David has to "discipline his heart," he is blind to Dora's limitations, he is full of illusions about her, they're completely mismatched. By the end of *David Copperfield*, it is very clear that David has to marry Agnes, for she represents David's achievement of maturity and self knowledge. But Dora challenges David in ways he will not understand until he is older, and in ways perfect Agnes never does. Dora structures part of his psychology. She is the woman who replaces his childish mother in his fantasy, and she is the object of conflicted emotions that turn out to be important to David's development—such as guilt. His depression after Dora's death feels insurmountable, he is almost suicidal. "I came to think that the Future was walled up before me, that the energy and action of my life were at an end, that I never could find any refuge but in the grave." (54) That is because he feels guilty, but this feeling is something he has to work through, it is constructive guilt, as Winnicott would say.[27] David Copperfield writes his third novel out of this experience.

And David has an important lesson to learn. He has to understand that Dora, also, has had something to endure in marriage, that she too has her heroism. To fear that you are always disappointing your beloved, to know that he would have been better with someone like Agnes, yet to accept that you cannot change enough to please him—this is a mature theme, and no doubt it happens often enough in life (I can imagine Catherine Dickens having had such thoughts). What touches me most is how both David and Dora keep tactfully to themselves their private feelings about their marriage. Moved by love and justice, they will not accuse or hurt each other. David never comes out and says to Dora, "I made the wrong choice, you are not the person to help me through life." Dora never says outright, "I will always disappoint you, and it pains me." When Dora dances with Jip and plays the guitar, when David buys her the cookery book and tries to form her mind, when she asks David to call her "child-wife," when he teases her about their unlucky choice of servants, the unsaid words *We have made a mistake* cast their shadow across their domestic gaiety, just as Annie Strong's words about "unsuitability in mind and purpose" echo through David's mind. (45) And what is heartbreaking to me is that Dora completely loves David, and he loves her, very genuinely, very dearly. And yet ...

The third "Retrospect," Chapter 53, is the shortest chapter by far in *David Copperfield*, only 1,978 words. Usually Dickens uses the present tense in the "Retrospect" chapters in order to fast-forward events: in Chapter 18, we rush through David's school days and his boyish infatuations, in Chapter 43 his wedding day is a hurried and incoherent dream. But in Chapter 53 time passes slowly, or so it feels to David. "All else grows dim, and fades away. I am again with Dora, in our cottage. I do not know how long she has been ill.

I am so used to it in feeling, that I cannot count the time. It is not really long, in weeks or months; but, in my usage and experience, it is a weary, weary while." "What a strange rest and pause in my life there seems to be," he says, "—and in all life, within doors and without—when I sit in the quiet, shaded, orderly room, with the blue eyes of my child-wife turned towards me, and her little fingers twining round my hand! Many and many an hour I sit thus; but, of all those times, three times come the freshest on my mind." (53)

The first time it is morning. David and Dora reminisce about their courtship and look to happy days ahead when she will be well. The second time it is evening, and Dora asks David to send for Agnes. The third time it is night. Dora and David are alone in her room. She tells him she may have been too young when they married. "I am afraid it would have been better, if we had only loved each other as a boy and girl, and forgotten it. I have begun to think I was not fit to be a wife," she tells him gently. "I was very happy, very. But, as years went on, my dear boy would have wearied of his child-wife. She would have been less and less a companion for him. He would have been more and more sensible of what was wanting in his home. She wouldn't have improved. It is better as it is." (53) Dora has finally given utterance, with great kindness and courage, to the truth as she has come to understand it through the short years of her marriage. But she has known it almost since the beginning of their courtship. Dora is not silly and stupid. She is observant, intuitive, she knows herself, and she knows David. After she meets Agnes for the first time, she says to him, "I wonder why you ever fell in love with me?" "I wondered what she was thinking about," David says cluelessly. (42) After their marriage she often looks at David with "quiet attention." He frequently wonders at her thoughtful moods. When David tries to form her mind, she knows exactly what is going on:

> "It's of not a bit of use," said Dora, shaking her head, until the ear-rings rang again. "You know what a little thing I am, and what I wanted you to call me from the first. If you can't do so, I am afraid you'll never like me. Are you sure you don't think, sometimes, it would have been better to have—"
> "Done what, my dear?" For she made no effort to proceed.
> "Nothing!" said Dora.
> "Nothing?" I repeated.
> She put her arms round my neck, and laughed, and called herself by her favourite name of a goose, and hid her face on my shoulder in such a profusion of curls that it was quite a task to clear them away and see it. (48)

There are so many moments like this between them, suppressed hints and loving evasions. Looking back, David now understands what they mean. He recollects them with tears in his eyes.

When Dora dies, David has been waiting downstairs while she speaks to Agnes alone in her room. Jip lies in his pagoda by the fire. Outside, the moon is bright. "As I look out on the night, my tears fall fast," David writes, "and my undisciplined heart is chastened heavily—heavily."

> I sit down by the fire, thinking with a blind remorse of all those secret feelings I have nourished since my marriage. I think of every little trifle between me and Dora, and feel the truth, that trifles make the sum of life. Ever rising from the sea of my remembrance, is the image of the dear child as I knew her first, graced by my young love, and by her own, with every fascination wherein such love is rich. Would it, indeed, have been better if we had loved each other as a boy and a girl, and forgotten it? Undisciplined heart, reply! (53)

Trifles make the sum of life. It is not a platitude, but sobering truth. Would it have been better to have loved Dora and forgotten it? She's the one who says it first, she wants to protect her husband from all that guilt. But their young love *has* graced their lives. And anyway, David would not have forgotten it. Dickens didn't. On February 10, 1855, he wrote to Maria Beadnell (now Mrs. Henry Winter), "Three or four and twenty years vanished like a dream, and I opened [your letter] with the touch of my young friend David Copperfield when he was in love."[28] In letter after letter, Dickens confessed to her how vividly he could recollect those emotions. They were important, more important than he could have known at that time in his young life. The secret feelings, the blind remorse, bring David to the edge of some crucial knowledge about his life. And maybe he is too hard on himself. Do most people choose rationally when they fall in love with someone, do they select the right partner the first time around? Undisciplined hearts, reply!

In *David Copperfield*, Dickens honestly explores what it feels like to truly love someone, to adore so many things about them, to be very happy with that person, and yet to wonder how it would have been with someone different. "I loved my wife dearly, and I was happy," David confesses, "but the happiness I had vaguely antici-pated, once, was not the happiness I enjoyed, and there was always something wanting." (48) Marriage, like everything, has its shades and degrees of happiness. David's marriage is not intolerably miserable—not as miserable as his aunt Betsey's was, or his mother's marriage to Murdstone. David's misgivings are occasional and speculative, and probably quite normal. "Between the two extremes—those who feel they retain creative living in marriage and those who are hampered in this respect by marriage—there is surely some kind of borderline," writes Winnicott, "and on this borderline very many of us happen to be situated. We are *happy enough*, and can be creative, but we do realize that there is inherently some kind of clash between the personal impulse and the compromises that belong to any kind of relationship that has reliable features."[29] But then why is there so much pressure to be happy, to keep checking in on how it's going? "Happy marriage is a concept I no longer accept without question anyway," writes Jane Tompkins, "the idea irks me; I don't see it as a normal, taken-for-granted occurrence or condition, like a good meal or a sunny day." The marriage is always there, but because it is always there, it can sometimes fade into the background of simply living. "Marriage is simultaneously a minute-to-minute and long term thing," as Tompkins puts it. "Who can say what it is?"[30]

When I married right out of college, barely 22 years old, I had a strong foreboding that I was making a mistake. My husband was a kind and decent person, but what I felt was not how I expected love to feel, and I knew from almost the very beginning that our minds and passions were not on the same track. We were *unsuitable*, as Annie Strong says—a word that covers it all. Our marriage did not last long.

For almost my whole life, I have been anti-marriage, not on principle, other people could marry as much as they liked, but marriage was not for me. As my feminist self reasoned, those gender roles were too strong for anyone, and there could be no true equality given that marriage is a patriarchal institution. (Before the United States legalized gay marriage, I didn't want to be part of an institution that discriminated against my friends and relatives, either. Or that was my excuse, anyway.) I liked my independence, living in my house with my things, following my own rhythms. I am a person who needs a lot of solitude, and the constant sociability of being married would grate on my nerves. Being married also looked like a lot of work—twice as much shopping, twice as much cooking, twice as much cleaning. Then I wondered if I could trust the man I married. Would he remain faithful to me? I couldn't stand the idea of my life becoming a soap opera of adultery, lies, accusations. I'd already been there. In my feverish little brain there was just something degrading about getting married. It was conformist, conventional, I'd be someone's *wife*, it didn't match my image of myself, and I just didn't want to! I was in a serious, relationship with a kind, smart man for almost 14 years. For 11 of those years we lived in separate cities, and we sometimes joked about how silly that was. Why didn't we just get married? But we could never bring ourselves to make a definite plan. Why? We were simpatico in so many ways—to be quite honest, Richard, ten years my senior, my former professor in graduate school, was the person who revealed Dickens's genius to me. Not only did we read Dickens together, but he fanned the flames of my Anglophilia by taking me to London to see the Dickens house for the first time, and to Rochester to see the Swiss Chalet, and to Gad's Hill, and even to Cooling to see the little stone lozenges from *Great Expectations* (not five, but 13!). Richard brought me to a meeting of the Dickens Society in Cleveland when I was a graduate student, at which I actually held in my hands a letter signed by Dickens. He understood all the Dickensian allusions I'd make in the course of normal conversation, so I never had to explain how funny I was being. He even wrote a truly excellent one-man play about Dickens. But a shared love of Dickens could not keep us together. That relationship ended, sadly and excruciatingly, when I was 43 and it felt like a divorce. Why didn't we try harder to work things out? Were we that unhappy? I do not know anymore, it's all gotten cloudy. But I know that after almost twenty years, I sometimes still feel torn, confused, and ashamed. As if I left an important book in an airport or a hotel somewhere just before I got to the crucial chapter, where everything is revealed. I would never know now how it was supposed to end.

A friend is putting together a cross-disciplinary lecture series at my university and wants me to present a talk alongside a music professor. I am not too enthused, but I agree to meet her and the other faculty member, a jazz composer and arranger, for a glass of wine. In rom-com movies and popular song, when destined strangers meet for the first time, their eyes lock across the room as though an electric force cut through the space between them. Does this happen when Charles, in faded t-shirt and shorts, strolls into the bar? I cannot be certain, but this is my impression. He has a delightful voice, a warm laugh, the brightest blue eyes, the pleasantest and most fascinating little ways that ever led a lost middle-aged woman into hopeless slavery. He is rather compact in build, and balding. So much the more precious, I think.

But we are not David and Dora, and modern love is complicated. After six years of testing the waters—proceed with caution!— on a cold, drenching day in November 2011 we drive eight hours from our town in central Virginia to Greenport, New York, a resort village on the North Fork of Long Island. I have never been to Long Island and know nothing about the lay of the land. I just want to find a place in the state of New York (gay marriage is legal here, for this is still my excuse) where I will feel anonymous and far away from everything. Greenport is at the extreme edge of the peninsula, and is deserted in the off-season. We settle in as Long Island tourists for a couple of days, and miraculously the November clouds clear, the weather turns unexpectedly temperate. We sit at a picnic table at a local winery, we walk on the beach, we drive around the swanky Hamptons on the other side of the island. We have made an appointment to be married on a Friday morning at the Greenport Town Hall. At last the day arrives. When we show up in our finery, we are asked to sit in an overheated room while a hearty woman in her 50s wearing a blue L.L. Bean jacket runs out to find the mayor. After a few minutes, Mayor David Nyce, a cheery, wiry Dickensian character in his early 40s with receding black hair tied in a ponytail, and three earrings, emerges from a back room in a red checkered lumberjack shirt and jeans held up by suspenders (he is engaged in a carpentry project), apologizing for forgetting our appointment. We shake hands heartily all around and take our places, and I am in a dream, a flustered, happy, hurried dream. I read aloud, with the gravest solemnity, the words on the small card Mayor Nyce has handed me, tears in my eyes, scared to death, then Charles reads his words, we are hugged by the two clerks, we take some snapshots with Mayor Nyce, I am crying, Charles is beaming, we walk out into the sunny autumn day, and it is over—for we have kept our marriage journey a secret from absolutely everyone. The next day we drive to Manhattan for our honeymoon and I awake from the dream, I believe it at last. As I begin to relax, as it begins to feel real, gratitude and contentment seep and warm and settle inside me. "Are you happy now, you foolish girl," head says to heart, "and sure you don't repent?"

"What readers want from reading and lovers want from love are experiences of a very similar design," writes Anne Carson. "It is a necessarily triangular design and it embodies a reach for the unknown....As you perceive the edge of yourself at the moment of desire, as you perceive the edges of words from moment to moment in reading (or writing) you are stirred to reach beyond perceptible edges—toward something else, something not yet grasped."[31] To read and to love are reaches of the imagination. To read and to love take time, in the Deep of time. Sometimes it is boring, sometimes it is very exciting indeed. To read and to love are day-to-day and forever, trifles and the sum of everything. To read and to love require trust and faith, because, as Carson puts it, "The words we read and the words we write never say exactly what we mean. The people we love are never just as we desire them."[32] Yet in our books and our loves, we gain proximity to something elementary that might warm us against the harsh winds of an indifferent world.

Carson thinks about reading and eros as sites of vitality, times when we feel alive: "Readers in real life, as well as within fiction, bear witness to the allure of the written text." She uses Dickens as an example:

> The novelist Eudora Welty says of her mother: "She read Dickens in the spirit in which she would have eloped with him." Dickens himself would not have been discomfited by such a spirit in a reader, if we may judge from a letter he wrote to Maria Beadnell in 1855. Here he speaks of his novel *David Copperfield* to the woman who inspired Dora: "Perhaps you have once or twice laid down that book and thought 'How dearly that boy must have loved me and how vividly this man remembers it!'" Through Francesca, through Tatiana, through Maria Beadnell, through Eudora Welty's mother, some current of eros leapt from a written page.[33]

When we read with that wide attention I mentioned earlier, when we let ourselves be surprised, let the author have his way with us, something may leap out. In marriage, too, if we have our eyes open, something may take a leap. To marry *is* to take a leap. So is writing, and opening a novel, and stepping into a classroom. I don't know what twist in the plot may be around the next bend. I live with fear and bated breath, apprehension and mild excitement—in chronic suspense for the dawn of every ordinary day in the extraordinary story that is my life.

"Not a deed of faithfulness or courage is done, except upon a maybe," says James.[34] "I have taken with fear and trembling to authorship," David confides. (43) That is a big leap for him, a big maybe. It pays off. By the time David is married to Dora, he can say "I pursued my vocation with confidence." (48) *Vocation*, from the Latin *vocare*, to call to service. And *David Copperfield* is Dickens's most passionate argument for the vocation of the artist in modern society, specifically for the novelist as the guardian and the instrument of love. In a once controversial polemic, *On Moral Fiction*, first published in 1978, John Gardner writes:

> For great art, even concern is not enough. Great art celebrates life's potential, offering a vision unmistakably and unsentimentally rooted in love. "Love" is of course another of those embarrassing words, perhaps a word even more embarrassing than "morality," but it's a word no aesthetician ought carelessly to drop from his vocabulary. Misused as it may be by pornographers and the makers of greeting-cards, it has, nonetheless, a firm, hard-headed sense that names the single quality without which true art cannot exist.[35]

Love is the motive force of great art. I think Dickens felt this was true. No, he knew it was true. He spoke often and openly about his love for his fictional "companions," "the creatures of my brain." (Preface). He sometimes shed tears when he wrote scenes of special pathos, he cried for Steerforth and Little Nell and little Paul Dombey. He believed in what he was writing because the stories really were, for Dickens, rooted in love.

Dickens loved *David Copperfield*, it was his "favorite child." But writing this so intimate novel stirred emotional susceptibilities that Dickens also found difficult to accept. As he wrote the last lines of the serial he was flooded with ambivalence. "I am within three pages of the shore; and am strangely divided, as is usual in such cases, between sorrow and joy," he wrote to Forster. "Oh, my dear Forster, if I were to say half of what Copperfield makes me feel to-night, how strangely, even to you, I should be turned inside out! I seem to be sending some part of myself into the Shadowy World."[36] As Dickens confessed in his 1850 Preface to *David Copperfield*,

> I do not find it easy to get sufficiently far away from this Book, in the first sensations of having finished it, to refer to it with the composure which this formal heading would seem to require. My interest in it, is so recent and strong; and my mind is so divided between pleasure and regret—pleasure in the achievement of a long design, regret in the separation from many companions—that I am in danger of wearying the reader whom I love, with personal confidences, and private emotions.

And the reader who is loved by Dickens thinks, Go ahead and weary me. Your story is really my story now. And I don't need to know everything.

A few years ago, one quiet summer afternoon, windows open, Rocky or Rascal probably still yapping in the distance, I was so engrossed in a novel that I practically leapt out of my skin when the phone rang. Was it that summer I was addictively reading

Edward St. Aubyn's Patrick Melrose novels? Or the summer I got lost in Carlos Ruiz Zafón's *The Shadow of the Wind*? I don't remember and it doesn't matter. The person who called me, the person I later married on the edge of Long Island at the age of 51, must have heard the startle in my voice. He asked if he'd interrupted anything. I said no, that I was just reading. "In the upstairs sleeping porch, with all the windows open, on the white couch, with your dog next to you," he said. That was eerily right in every detail. "I know," he said complacently. "I can just picture you."

3

THE SHADOW FELL
LIKE LIGHT

According to the American Psychological Association, in 2020 more than three-quarters of Americans (77%) said the country's future is "a significant source of stress," up from 66% in 2019.[1] This study followed the dozens and dozens of articles in mainstream media since the 2016 presidential election about how depressed people were. We were suffering from "post-election grief" and "Trump-related anxiety." Vox reported that in the four years of his term in office, Donald Trump subjected people to "the language and tactics used by abusers," including gaslighting, explosive anger, lying, and seeking revenge for perceived wrongs.[2] People I knew confessed they were experiencing real anguish and confusion. Some, despairing for the future, wanted to find a way to leave the country. It was like a subterranean current of worry and distress was pulling everyone down. We bravely sallied forth to carry out our day-to-day responsibilities, trying to resist or ignore the toxicity of the Trump regime. But deep down it was hard not feel hopeless.

In the months after Donald Trump became president, instead of trying to stay informed by the experts on CNN or MSNBC, which was too depressing, I listened to some weekly podcasts called "Speaking of Jung," where psychoanalysts conversed apocalyptically about the repressed collective shadow that was stalking us—which was also depressing. Though it felt bizarre to hear someone discussing political events in terms of symbols, dreams, and archetypes, I felt more at home here than with mainstream media. The speakers in the podcast did not pretend to know what was going on politically, they were not pundits. They were observers of something both familiar and ominous, and they wanted to make sense of it within their special frame of reference. As D. W. Winnicott observed, "Unconscious feelings may sway bodies of people at critical moments, and who is to say that this is bad or good? It is just a fact, and one that has to be taken into account all the time by rational politicians if nasty shocks are to be avoided."[3] Maybe psychoanalytical thinking could have saved the nation a nasty shock—it certainly sounded like those Jungians saw it coming. And though their prognostications were very grim indeed, they did not sound panicked. These intelligent, articulate people gave me the sense that something was taking its course in world history, slouching towards Bethlehem again. I just happened to be alive during this particular madness.

Some "Speaking of Jung" contributors proffered theories about the rise of dictators at different cycles of history, the allure of delusional leaders, and the Trump persona. Some spoke about the emotional momentum of being in large groups, how masses of people submerge the individual and bring forth the shadow. More than one speaker suggested that there are deep-seated reasons in the American psyche for the ascendancy of a bully like Trump. Maybe people felt inadmissible shame, or grieved the loss of a connection to something sacred and vital in their lives and needed someone to blame: the educated liberals with satisfying jobs, the environmentalists who didn't care about jobs, the immigrants who took Americans' jobs away from them. Probably not everyone was looking for a scapegoat, though. People can feel trapped, by government ineptitude, unfulfilling work, broken relationships. They were just not doing well. Life was not turning out as they were promised. Maybe it was nobody's fault.

World events challenge the understanding. What I liked about the Jungians was that they recognized that there are also challenges to the heart and the psyche. People get lost, so so lost. We get stuck on what's out there in the world and ignore the demands of the inner life. The psyche takes revenge by distorting that world, and "you read with gusto the lies of atrocity-mongers and pass them on to your friends as if they were external truth."[4] The price to pay, says Winnicott, is not growing as individuals, "just staying as we are, playthings of economics and of politics and of fate." Soul-imprisonment, false selves, lives worn away by guilt and lies, by following the wrong rules and rulers. Nothing moves forward, nothing matures. And so, inevitably, people "caught up in the prison of the rigidity of their own defences will try to destroy freedom."[5]

The society Dickens presents in *Little Dorrit* does not, in any of its particulars, look like my society in the first quarter of the twenty-first century. We don't have debtors' prisons and Dickens didn't have Twitter. Yet there is something—the sense of unrest, antipathy, even spitefulness—that Dickens comprehends about social life that is recognizable, even from this distance. In *Little Dorrit*, no one storms federal buildings, police officers do not murder Black citizens, no one drives a car into a crowded public square. But people are psychologically aggressive, determined at all costs to hold their position, to give no ground. The aggression is usually disguised as something else, but that doesn't make it less frightening. Characters push aside unpleasant truths, revise facts, inhabit a version of reality that suits their ambitions. Let me offer some examples.

First, the women. Mrs. Merdle, with her prominent bosom, is the "Priestess of Society." Her totem is a caged parrot with "scaly legs" and a "cruel beak and black tongue" that shrieks and laughs and trails itself grotesquely outside its golden cage in Mrs. Merdle's drawing room. The Dowager Mrs. Gowan, a toady and hanger-on, is Mrs. Merdle's friend. She lives in Hampton Court, a scrubby, dog-eared, vulgar neighborhood which the residents pretend is cultured and bohemian: arched passageways pretend to be dining rooms, coal-cellars pretend to be walls, curtains pretend not to be hiding a bed. Mrs. Gowan and Mrs. Merdle have decided that it is a concession of the Family greatness to allow Henry Gowan to marry Minnie Meagles. Mrs. Merdle "perceiving the exact nature of the fiction to be nursed ... put her required contribution of gloss upon it."[6] Together, these women invent some alternative facts that become the official version of the marriage circulated at large in society. No one questions its truth.

Mrs. General, hired by Mr. Dorrit for a ridiculous fee to act as companion to Fanny and Amy when the family travel abroad, does not allow anyone to see anything about the world that does not conform to her concept of respectability. Her job is to "varnish" the surface of everything. When Mrs. General is "in her pure element," nobody has an opinion, there is no free thought or free speech. "Nothing disagreeable should ever be looked at," she instructs Amy. Mrs. General is "transcendently genteel," a precise description of all of these women, mummified by their manners, clothes, and cosmetics, intent on seeing only what they want to see. (2.5) Mr. F's Aunt is one of Dickens's oddest inventions, but she too has her part in the charade. If Mrs. General is the ego, Mr. F's Aunt is the id. "Give him a meal of chaff!" "Bring him for'ard, and I'll chuck him out o' winder!" (2.9, 2.34) Her senile outbursts amplify and externalize the covert violence of the other women.

Fanny Dorrit is spiteful, spoiled, greedy, and insensitive. When people do not accommodate her wishes, she whines "I wish I were dead!" She marries Mrs. Merdle's son, Sparkler, because she wants to get back at Mrs. Merdle for slighting her, to make her feel old and take her down a notch. Fanny plays her haughty role determinedly. When she seals her fate by accepting Sparkler's proposal, she weeps in her sister Amy's arms, "the last time Fanny ever showed that there was any hidden, suppressed, or conquered feeling in her on the matter. From that hour the way she had chosen lay before her, and she trod it with her own imperious self-willed step." (2.14) Then there is Miss Wade. She does not conceal her aggression from others. On the contrary, she hates out in the open, and even keeps a written record of her corrosive desire for revenge. Some people organize their sense of self around negative emotions, and Miss Wade, like Rosa Dartle and Uriah Heep, is one of these people.

Now the men. Christopher Casby is called the Patriarch. He exudes an aura of gentle authority: "What with his blooming face, and that head, and his blue eyes, he seemed to be delivering sentiments of rare wisdom and virtue. In like manner, his physiognomical expression seemed to teem with benignity. Nobody could have said where the wisdom was, or where the virtue was, or where the benignity was; but they all seemed to be somewhere about him." (1.13) His innate viciousness comes out when he orders Pancks to squeeze the tenants of Bleeding-Heart Yard: "You are paid to squeeze, and you must squeeze to pay." (2.32) Then there is the villainous Rigaud Blandois, who struts, or slithers, through European cities, ingratiating, full of "smiling politeness." (2.1) The devil is a gentleman, and he is at large in the world. "In this novel about the will and society," wrote Lionel Trilling, "the devilish nature of Blandois is confirmed by his maniac insistence upon his gentility, his mad reiteration that it is the right and necessity of his existence to be served by others."[7] Rigaud assumes that anyone of any importance will recognize *his* importance. Henry Gowan finds him useful. Amy, Minnie, and Gowan's dog, Lion, have an instinctive antipathy to him.

The Circumlocution Office is hilariously funny, of course, but Dickens conveys with determination how damaging to people is its bureaucratic nonchalance. Mr. Tite Barnacle is its representative, "the express image and presentment of How not to do it." (1.10) He is practically straitjacketed: "He wound and wound folds of white cravat round his neck, as he wound and wound folds of tape and paper round the neck of the country. His wristbands and collar were oppressive; his voice and manner were oppressive. He had a large watch-chain and bunch of seals, a coat buttoned up to inconvenience, a waistcoat buttoned up to inconvenience, an unwrinkled pair of trousers, a stiff pair of boots. He was altogether splendid, massive, overpowering, and impracticable." (1.10) Arthur Clennam can get nothing out of him, "It being one of the principles of the Circumlocution Office never, on any account whatever, to give a straightforward answer." (1.10) This is a particularly maddening form of domination, one with which most of us are quite familiar.

Henry Gowan's cynical attitude about art and the vocation of the artist is, to Dickens, especially profane (in this character,

Dickens may be taking a stab at Thackeray). Gowan calls himself "a disappointed man," and he laughs at Arthur's idea that an artist is bound to uphold his vocation, "and to claim for it the respect it deserves." Gowan sighs that he wishes he could "live in such a rose-coloured mist. But what I do in my trade, I do to sell. What all we fellows do, we do to sell. If we didn't want to sell it for the most we can get for it, we shouldn't do it. Being work, it has to be done; but it's easily enough done. All the rest is hocus-pocus." (1.34) Gowan, like Mrs. Merdle, wants everyone to think he's condescended to the Meagles, who are a step down socially, while *he* is related to the Barnacles. He generally succeeds in this. Young men who are not outwardly mendacious or threatening are merely inconsequential. Edmund Sparkler is mentally feeble. Tip Dorrit is "tired of everything," less manipulative than Henry Gowan only because he is less intelligent. (1.7) His one saving grace is his affection for his sister Amy. All the young Barnacles are weak and silly.

Finally, there is Mr. Merdle, the great capitalist and fraud. He is always "slinking" in and out of the splendid rooms in his splendid house, "with his hands crossed under his uneasy coat-cuffs, clasping his wrists as if he were taking himself into custody." (1.33) Merdle doesn't look well. There were "black traces on his lips where they met as if a little train of gunpowder had been fired there." (2.16) Physician decides that Mr. Merdle has a "deep-seated recondite complaint," but he cannot quite diagnose it. "Mr. Merdle's complaint. Society and he had so much to do with one another in all things else, that it is hard to imagine his complaint, if he had one, being solely his own affair." (1.21) When he knows the game is up and that his swindling has ruined thousands of lives, he cuts his throat in a Turkish bath with the dark-handled penknife he earlier borrowed from his daughter-in-law, Fanny.

Dickens is angry. The lies and fictions these characters devise are profoundly damaging, and profoundly sad. William Dorrit, especially, is a most pitiful man, the Willy Loman of the Victorian period, and attention must be paid. But the others, the Gowans and Merdles and Casbys—what a world Dickens puts them in. So fake, so empty. There is something almost pathological about people's defensive facades in *Little Dorrit*, as though society had a collective narcissistic neurosis. Everyone is looking for someone to lord it over so they can keep running in big, important, ever-expanding circles. Just running and running.

Every Wednesday for 14 weeks between January and May 2015, I met with nine undergraduate students from 5:00 to 8:00 pm in a small third-floor classroom to talk about Dickens. The climate control in the room had a mind of its own, it was either freezing or so humid it smelled like a locker room, and the makeshift furniture made it a tight fit even for nine people. But to compensate, the large west-facing window offered pretty views of the sun going down over the Blue Ridge mountains. As I asked my questions about Dickens, I covertly watched the pigeons fluttering on the tile roof, the setting sun staining the chalkboard grayish pink. In January and February, when the class started at 5:00, it was almost dark. By the time it ended three hours later, we could see the moon. Soon the spring equinox gave us longer, lighter days—that year, the first day of spring coincided with a supermoon and a total solar eclipse. When the semester began, I walked home from the seminar in the cold and semi-darkness, under the yellow shadows of streetlights. By the end, the sky was lightly blue, the air fragrant with pear blossoms.

A three-hour class on Dickens can be draining for all parties, and I am not a ball of energy even at my best. But there was something going on with me that restless season. It wasn't just nervousness about politics, I wasn't paying serious attention to Donald Trump back then. It was underneath me, or inside of me. I felt tired and unmoored. There was turbulence in my marriage that I did not understand, more quarrels, less closeness and listening. We had only been married four years and I didn't know if we would make it. In my deepest center I felt embattled. It may seem an exaggeration, but privately I felt I was fighting to survive. I felt trapped by my life, depressed and discouraged, and I did not know why. There were evenings I would walk home at night from my Dickens seminar as if in a haze, all I wanted was my dog and my glass of wine, to disappear, to sleep. I suppose I had finally made my way into the middle of that dark wood.

When I was 34, my lovely friend Claire, who was then in her 70s, presented me with a book written by a friend of hers entitled *The Middle Passage: From Misery to Meaning in Midlife*. The author, James Hollis, was a former English professor who left academia after 25 years to study Analytical Psychology at the C. G. Jung Institute outside of Zurich. He was now a certified analyst, and *The Middle Passage* was his first book. *The Middle Passage* sat neglected on my shelf for almost ten years. I didn't think it applied to me (34 did not count as midlife in my estimation of things). The man I was with at the time, the Dickens lover, had read it but *he* was ten years older, or so I vainly reasoned. When I finally got around to *The Middle Passage*, that relationship had ended, and I was "on the high seas and alone." I read this short book slowly over a weekend in the quiet and solitude of a Washington hotel room in January 2004. It was almost an awakening. I think I liked all the poetry and literature this former English professor cited as much as anything. He seemed especially to love Rilke:

I live my life in growing orbits
which move out over the things of the world.
Perhaps I can never achieve the last,
but that will be my attempt.
I am circling around God, around the ancient tower,
and I have been circling for a thousand years,
and I still don't know if I am a falcon, or a storm,
or a great song.[8]

I too felt I was circling, endlessly circling, like David Copperfield's rooks. I was feeling the Deep of time, fearing mistakes I had made, wanting to be a better person. I don't know what I was after, but Hollis gave me a frame for my emotions, he opened a door for me. A few years later, I started reading books by Jung, Freud, Winnicott, Milner, Bachelard, Alice Miller, Christopher Bollas, and Adam Phillips, books about object-relations theory, psychoanalysis and reading, the sources of creativity, the therapeutic process, childhood, selfhood. I read with reckless abandon, without any plan or chronology, without a classroom or a community. How I wish I had known about this intellectual world when I was younger. If I had started earlier, I would have had something to build on. I am sure I did not understand half of what I read, not clinically for certain. Some of these books were written by and for psychoanalysts. Yet, just maybe, something was getting through.

There seems to be a disproportionately large number of social workers and mental health professionals in my small town, but I had to hunt to find one who had experience with depth psychology. Patricia was about seventy and had had a successful career in group and organizational counseling in another state. She was now back in Virginia, studying to be a psychoanalyst at the Jung Institute, going through analysis herself, and incrementally working towards her certificate. When I called her, she had one slot left in her schedule. I booked an appointment for the next day. I'd been in counseling before, the cognitive therapy type, but I did not stay with it for long because it always felt superficial. "Why am I paying someone when I could just read George Eliot," I remember thinking. But I had no experience with the kind of therapy that goes to the root, and I was both eager and apprehensive. I was seeking the meaning of my malaise, I wanted to stare into the chasm. But I was also afraid of what I might find down there.

I saw Patricia every other week for a little over five years. I know psychotherapy is not for everyone and many people are skeptical of it. But the whole process was intensely fascinating to me. Adam Phillips says somewhere that analysis is a little like literary criticism, and this is how I saw it at first. I had an intellectual interest in what Patricia and I were doing together. I took notes, sometimes I even brought books I'd read to our session, or poems—when I was teaching Dickens, I talked to her about what I was seeing in his novels. (*Does reading all this Dickens affect the vividness of my dreams?* I wrote in my journal that April.) In preparation for each session, I started to write down my dreams, and we tried Active Imagination and other Jungian exercises. I liked the writing assignments and the storytelling, and my brain was excited to make connections—the reflex of a life in academia. But as I was soon to learn, thinking was not entirely what this kind of therapy was about.

I noticed, after several months, that one thing we kept circling back to was my guardedness. Patricia wondered if was I hiding. "You like to disappear," she said one day. This took me by surprise: just the week before I had been writing in my journal about a visit to my family in Cleveland that had upset me, even though nothing had happened specifically, everyone was their usual jovial selves.

It's the group thing that wears me out, I wrote in my diary. *I like disappearing.* Now here was Patricia using the very word I had used. I asked what she meant. She pointed out how I make myself small, speak quietly, write in the tiniest script. Why do I drink, why do I love to sleep? Why do I keep back certain emotions, especially anger? "You're *secretive*," Richard once told me. "I'm just a private person," I said, defensively. But now I wondered. *Was* I secretive? Why? What was I holding onto, what was I shielding from others, from myself? Patricia helped me to understand aspects of my childhood that might have made me want to hide, and also to see how other people, especially those I loved the most, often made it difficult for me to summon the energy to claim a space for myself. For I really did not want to hide at all. I wanted desperately to be seen. What Winnicott wrote is so very true: "*It is joy to be hidden but disaster not to be found.*"[9]

The spikes of the Marshalsea Prison cast their shadows across many pages of *Little Dorrit*. "What place is this?" asks Arthur Clennam, as crowds of people push past him. The prison is a banal fact to the busy populace outside its gates. Nobody has time for it. London is loud and alienating, crowded, suffocatingly busy. Crowds are *throngs*, the great thoroughfares *roar*, the streets are *turbulent* and *boisterous*. People are everywhere. "In Dickens's universe," observes Rosemarie Bodenheimer, "it is virtually impossible to be alone." Even when characters are by themselves they're watched by shadowy eyes, spied upon by houses, furniture, or phantoms. Bodenheimer thinks Dickens used this "power of animation" to ward off his fear of isolation. This is certainly true. When he visited American prisons in 1842, Dickens recorded his horror at the idea of solitary confinement, vividly imagining "the immense amount of torture and agony which this dreadful punishment, prolonged of years, inflicts upon the sufferers."[10] Projecting his own worst nightmares onto the prisoners he saw, Dickens was certain they must see specters. In his biography of Dickens, John Forster wrote,

> ...Dickens's childish sufferings, and the sense they burnt into him of the misery of loneliness and a craving for joys of home, though they led to what was weakest in him, led also to what was greatest. It was his defect as well as his merit in maturer life not to be able to live alone. When the fancies of his novels were upon him and he was under their restless influence, though he often talked of shutting himself up in out of the way solitary places, he never went anywhere unaccompanied by members of his family.[11]

Dickens took his entourage with him whenever he traveled abroad, maintaining the habits of his domestic life in all the foreign cities he visited. When he shut himself in a room every day between breakfast and lunch to write his novels, members of the family were always within reach. Someone so afraid of abandonment truly must have had "burnt into him," in Forster's phrase, an experience of frightening aloneness.

And yet, *it is joy to be hidden*. This Dickens also knew. His self-preoccupation was intense. He was deeply curious about the mystery of his inventions, the daemon within that brought forth his stories. "It is the pen which dreams," writes Bachelard, and Dickens was one of the greatest dreamers in the world.[12] He used writing, as he used mesmerism, to observe the undulations of his psyche. Something was playing out, and he let it unspool, he dared himself. But only so far. In the Autobiographical Fragment, Dickens writes:

> The deep remembrance of the sense I had of being utterly neglected and hopeless, of shame I felt in my position, of the misery it was to my young heart to believe that, day by day, what I had learned, and thought, and delighted in, and raised my fancy and my emulation up by, was passing away from me, never to be brought back any more; cannot be written.[13]

Yet it *was* written. As John Carey observes, Dickens, "goes on writing this fragment of autobiography in novel after novel."[14] Forster aptly noted that when Dickens wrote *David Copperfield* he took "all the world into his confidence," by "sufficiently [disguising] himself under cover of his hero."[15] He was telling and not telling.

Many ordinary people are torn between wanting someone to know who they are and wanting to hide a secret self from the probing eyes of the world. Winnicott claimed, "At the centre of each person is an incommunicado element, and this is most sacred and worthy of preservation."[16] For artists, the conflict between hiding and being found can be the source of their creative energy. "In the artist of all kinds I think one can detect an inherent dilemma," writes Winnicott, "…the urgent need to communicate and the still more urgent need not to be found. This might account for the fact that we cannot conceive of an artist's ever coming to the end of the task that occupies his whole nature."[17] This seems to me a perfect description of an artist such as Dickens. Despite his public voice and his social criticism, he was *always* writing about himself, about something deeply personal and psychologically inviolable—prisons and shoe blacking peek out of his fictions as early as *Pickwick*. Dickens rescued and nursed his memories, dug them up like archeological fragments, raised them quickly to the light and then buried them again under the rippleless surface of his success. In Freud's idiom, Dickens suffered from reminiscences. But maybe he needed to suffer. The artist Louise Bourgeois notes in one of her journals:

> Some of us are so obsessed with the past that we die of it. It is the attitude of the poet who never finds the lost heaven and it is really the situation of artists who work for a reason nobody can quite grasp. They might want to reconstruct something of the past to exorcise it. It is that the past for certain people has such a hold and such a beauty . . .[18]

The stain and beauty of the past, Warren's Blacking and the Marshalsea Prison, his impecunious family, Maria Beadnell and his broken heart, they were part of Dickens's psychic architecture, they were "integral objects." The past can become a dangerous obsession, yes, we can get stuck there. But it may also be put to use. The "unconscious discovery of the integral object may allow for passionate usage of the object, and transform the negative energy of obsession into the positive energy of passion."[19] Something in Dickens was vitally sustained by his childhood experiences, as painful as they were. For they belonged only to him. They could explain so much.

Imagine two gentle people who have survived difficult childhoods. They are at separate points in life's winding journey, tossed and swayed by the demands and interference of others. In the extreme weariness of middle age and the repressed eroticism of youth, they sit alone and stare out of windows, gazing up at the stars, so distant and out of reach. They walk through a labyrinth of dirty streets, tuck themselves into dark corners and rented rooms, come together briefly in stifling chambers or on shadowy bridges.

They circle each other, not from wariness but from timidity. From not knowing what in their hearts they know.

Little Dorrit is Dickens's novel about inwardness, of what happens inside—inside the walls of the Marshalsea, inside the self. It is a novel about containment, and also about bringing what we know in our hearts out of its hiding place for another to see. It is almost miraculous that in a world so loud and indifferent, Amy Dorrit and Arthur Clennam find each other, that they see and listen to each other. Or they try to—there are encrusted layers of repressed emotion to get through, and an almost fatally weakened resolve, especially in forty-something Arthur. "I have no will," he tells Mr. Meagles.

> "That is to say,"—he coloured a little,—"next to none that I can put in action now. Trained by main force; broken, not bent; heavily ironed with an object on which I was never consulted and which was never mine; shipped away to the other end of the world before I was of age, and exiled there until my father's death there, a year ago; always grinding in a mill I always hated; what is to be expected from me in middle life? Will, purpose, hope? All those lights were extinguished before I could sound the words." (1.2)

"Light 'em up again!" says Mr. Meagles cheerfully. Dear, practical Mr. Meagles. To lighten up, to remake the future, to rekindle your soul—the breathtaking quests of middle-age.

"It was a girl, surely, whom I saw near you," Arthur asks Affery on his first night home, "—almost hidden in the dark corner?" "Oh! She? Little Dorrit? *She*'s nothing," Affery replies. (1.3) But Arthur observes her. She is "so little and light, so noiseless and shy, and appeared so conscious of being out of place among the three hard elders..." (1.5) He notices, in this family full of secrets, that there is an unusual shade of interest in Mrs. Clennam's treatment of Little Dorrit. He notices that "Little Dorrit let herself out to do needle-work. At so much a day—or at so little—from eight to eight, Little Dorrit was to be hired. Punctual to the moment, Little Dorrit appeared; punctual to the moment, Little Dorrit vanished. What became of Little Dorrit between the two eights was a mystery." He wonders about her: "But Little Dorrit?" He "watched for her, saw or did not see her, and speculated about her." He resolves "to watch Little Dorrit and know more of her story," and so he traces her to the Marshalsea, in a game of hide and seek. (1.5) But what is it he is seeking?

Mrs. Clennam tells Amy that Arthur has "an empty place in his heart that he has never known the meaning of." (2.31) Freud's entire science starts there. Arthur hardly understands what it is he wants. A woman? Could be. The very night he returns to his mother's house, he's thinking about falling in love. When Affery tells him that Flora is now a widow, it introduces "into the web that his mind was busily weaving, in that old workshop where the loom of his youth had stood, the last thread wanting to the pattern." (1.3) (In Dickens's Preface to *Little Dorrit*, he refers to holding the threads and "weaving" his story until the pattern is finished.) Minnie Meagles's pretty face had reminded Arthur of young Flora's, had "soared out of his gloomy life into the bright glories of fancy." (1.3) Sometimes the unconscious drops hints. On February 9, 1855, a servant placed a bundle of notes and correspondence on a table as Dickens sat reading by the fire. He looked briefly through them, found nothing there from anyone he knew, and went back to reading his book. "But," he writes, "I found my mind curiously disturbed, and wandering away through so many years to such early times of my life, that I was quite perplexed to account for it. There was nothing in what I had been reading, or immediately thinking about, to awaken such a train of thought, and at last it came into my head that it must have been suggested by something in the look of one of those letters."[20] He had recognized Maria Beadnell's handwriting.

In the folly of his youth, Arthur had "heaped upon [Flora] all the locked-up wealth of his affection and imagination. That wealth had been, in his desert home, like Robinson Crusoe's money; exchangeable with no one, lying idle in the dark to rust, until he poured it out for her."(1.12) (Dickens wrote to Maria in 1855 about the feelings "locked up in my own breast" that he could not share with anyone.[21]) When Arthur meets Flora (when Dickens met Maria), twenty years have passed for both of them. She is stout, "short of breath," "diffuse and silly." The experience is a "fatal blow" to Arthur's fantasy, excruciatingly painful. (1.13) He is dying to escape from the Casby home. But he accepts Flora's invitation to stay for dinner as "atonement"—and here is Dickens's honesty— for "the disappointment he almost felt ashamed of." (1.13)

After this disquieting visit, Arthur walks back to his lodgings. He sits by the dying fire, thinking of the setbacks in his life. He's not bitter. Arthur "was a man who had, deep-rooted in his nature, a belief in all the gentle and good things his life had been without," he is "a dreamer, after all" (1.13, 1.3). As the child of art and love, as Trilling says, Arthur has a special claim.[22] Though he was raised with a "restraining and correcting hand," Mrs. Clennam remembers that as a boy, he would look up at her from his books with "his mother's face…trying to soften me with his mother's ways." (2.131) So on this night of letdowns, sensitive Arthur dreams by the fire, reviewing his long, bare, blank life. But blankness and depression may sometimes be a prelude to integration and understanding.

> "From the unhappy suppression of my youngest days, through the rigid and unloving home that followed them, through my departure, my long exile, my return, my mother's welcome, my intercourse with her since, down to the afternoon of this day with poor Flora," said Arthur Clennam, "what have I found!"
>
> His door was softly opened, and these spoken words startled him, and came as if they were an answer:
>
> "Little Dorrit." (1.13)

The Christmas after we got married, Charles gave me a roundtrip ticket to London to celebrate my first ever sabbatical in the spring of 2012. I would have one week in March alone in London, to do whatever I wanted. It was a completely surprising, touching gift, for it came after many pre-marital conversations about finding a balance in our relationship in which we could each grow, where one person did not have to be subservient to the other's ambitions or tastes or rhythms. For 11 years, throughout my 30s, I lived alone and liked it. Ever since my twenties, my romantic ideal had been the relationship between Mary Wollstonecraft and William Godwin, two radicals and intellectuals who lived and worked in separate dwellings. Yet look how passionate they were! I was into Rilke's idea of love, from *Letters to a Young Poet*, that "two solitudes protect and border and greet each other."[23] I also liked to quote Dorothy Parker's quip, "When the two become one, I wonder which one they become?"[24] But if I had a fear of engulfment, Charles had a fear of abandonment. The household he grew up in was the opposite of my welcoming Italian-American family. He told me he never saw his parents kiss. His mother, Helen, seemed chronically angry.

His father, Jack, worked nights at the radio station he owned and so usually slept until afternoon. Helen had to be the enforcer, and raising four young boys largely on her own, she would run out of patience. It was a stable enough environment, and Charles has told me he never doubted his parents loved him. But it was not an especially warm home. Only much later, a year or so before Jack died, did Charles learn that his father had been taken away from his birth mother by the Catholic Church and placed in an institution for illegitimate children where he was cared for until he was almost three years old. Did Jack have problems attaching because of this experience? He never, ever spoke about his childhood, and we think he was deeply ashamed. After his death we learned that there was a period in his marriage where he had had a series of affairs (hence Helen's chronic rage). Charles, the first born, wanted his parents' attention, wanted to please them, like all children, yet he picked up on their bitterness and their resentments. Maybe Jack and Helen were so embroiled in their own emotions they didn't see how lonely he was. He has told me that when he was little, he would slip out of bed at night and sit outside his parents' room to hear the comforting hum of their air-conditioner. Extroverted, band-leader Charles likes to feel he's in charge. But periodically he feels overwhelmed by emptiness, a sense of acute forlornness. He wonders if he did not get enough of something as a child, stroking, touching, holding? It is as though he always wants more. Yet he doesn't want to keep searching for that magical other to make him feel fulfilled—the "magical other," of course, from *The Middle Passage*, which I bought for Charles the first year we were dating. Does Charles have "an empty place in his heart that he has never known the meaning of"?

In London, I imagined I would spend most of my afternoons in the big art galleries. But for some reason, other than the V&A,

I didn't feel like going to them. I spent afternoons walking around those quiet residential squares in central London, just drifting in circles. And I went to houses—the Sir John Soane's Museum, and the Dickens House just before it closed for renovations in preparation for Dickens's bicentenary. On my last Saturday I decided to trek out to Hampstead. I wanted to walk through Highgate Cemetery and see the famous graves (I learned later that Dickens's parents are buried there). And I wanted to visit the Freud Museum, the last house Freud lived in after he fled Austria in 1938. I wanted to see the couch.

Map in hand (this was before smartphones), I planned my journey by Underground and bus. Highgate Cemetery was not too hard to find. But 20 Maresfield Gardens eluded me. I walked in a circle all around the outside of the cemetery. I walked in residential areas, I walked through the village, I think I even walked across Hampstead Heath. What should have been a straightforward 30-minute walk turned into an exhausting odyssey. When I stopped people to ask about the Freud Museum or Maresfield Gardens, they listened and smiled politely as though I were quite mad. On a hunch, I hopped aboard a bus. It was so packed with Saturday shoppers I could barely reach a hand strap. But in the squeeze of people, a middle-aged man took pity on me as I tried to read my map without my glasses, and advised me in a soft Indian accent at which stop to get off. "The sailor cannot see the North— but knows the Needle can—"[25] When I got off the bus, something pointed me up a hill, around a crescent, through a leafy, peaceful neighborhood of postal carriers and dog-walkers to number 20.

In addition to the exhibits about Freud and Anna Freud, the museum had recently launched an exhibit on Louise Bourgeois called "The Return of the Repressed." I knew a little about

Bourgeois. She had died just two years before, in 2010, and I had read some articles about her and seen a short documentary. I remembered seeing *Spider* in the National Gallery of Art's Sculpture Garden in Washington, and the wonderful, huge *Maman* spider at the National Gallery of Art in Ottawa. The exhibit at the Freud Museum included many drawings, sculptures, and recently discovered letters and journals from the years she underwent psychoanalysis. So after I walked around Freud's library and saw the couch and the artefacts, I went upstairs to check out the Louise Bourgeois exhibit.

Bourgeois's art can feel confrontational, and some disturbing, emotionally raw works were on display. As I was going up to the next level of the exhibit, I was drawn to one work in particular, which I have never forgotten. It was displayed alone on a small landing up from a flight of stairs, light from a bay window streaming in behind it: the figure of a kneeling woman, a faceless fabric doll, with her head lowered and her breasts resting on a blood-red glass orb she holds encircled in her arms. The figure is inside a bell jar (Figure 3.1).

I stood looking at this sculpture from the step I was standing on for what seems many minutes, for it stopped me in my tracks, it was so beautiful, and so sad. I saw a woman holding something cherished and beloved. The vivid redness of the marble ball made it heavy and intense, but it was so close to her body, it seemed she was protecting it. At the same time, the glass jar was protecting her, preserving the privacy and sanctity of her relationship. Or was she imprisoned there, a Sleeping Beauty in her glass coffin, like one of the hanging puppets in Bourgeois's *Cell* series, also in the exhibit? She was alone with this precious thing—a memory? a wish? a shame?—and the space surrounding her in that sunny

Figure 3.1 Louise Bourgeois, *The Dangerous Obsession*, 2003. Fabric, glass, stainless steel and wood 56 1/2 × 24 × 20"; 143.5 × 60.9 × 50.8 cm. Photo: Christopher Burke, © 2021 The Easton Foundation, Licensed by VAGA at Artists Rights Society (ARS), NY

room seemed to praise and validate her. Yet there was unmistakable sadness. When I stepped closer, I could read the work's title: *The Dangerous Obsession*.

The image and the words lingered in my mind long after I returned home. I looked for it online and made it my computer's desktop image. I showed it to Patricia when I started therapy. *The Dangerous Obsession*. What did it mean? My feelings about it should have been enough, but the academic in me needed an art expert. Yet when I looked up what art critics had to say about this sculpture, there was no consensus. One said it was about motherhood and conveyed "wonder" at the life the woman has created, but also perhaps "fear and trepidation." Another suggested it showed "an awareness of the damage inflicted by clinging to past torments." Yet another thought it referred to "the creative process" that takes over an artist's life. One critic said it was about "being fixated on something lost or unobtainable, possibly an object of love" and "the danger of this psychological state and…its consequences of melancholy, and possibly even insanity."[26] Insanity? But how could it mean that, when it felt so beautiful and complete? When she was so quiet, so contained.

A King had a daughter. She was wise, beautiful, quick at her lessons, and she had "the power of knowing secrets." Near her Palace there was a cottage where a poor tiny woman lived all alone. One day the Princess saw the tiny woman spinning at her wheel, and she stopped at the cottage and asked: "Where do you keep it?" For the tiny woman had a secret: she kept the shadow of Some one in "a very secret place." The Princess asked to see it and the tiny woman timidly agreed.

> It was the shadow of Some one who had gone by long before: of Some one who had gone on far away quite out of reach, never, never to come back. It was bright to look at; and when the tiny woman showed it to the Princess, she was proud of it with all her heart, as a great, great treasure. When the Princess had considered it a little while, she said to the tiny woman, And you keep watch over this every day? And she cast down her eyes, and whispered, Yes. Then the Princess said, Remind me why. (1.24)

Amy Dorrit's story about the Princess and the tiny woman could be an allegory of psychoanalysis. The tiny woman has *a secret*; the Princess, like an analyst, knows and asks to see it. The tiny woman shows her. And the secret is *a shadow*. Strangely, this shadow is *bright to look at.* So it is not a mean or guilty secret. In fact, Amy's shadow is a *great great treasure,* one that she will take with her to her grave. Young Arthur's love for Flora, too, is described as "the locked-up wealth of his affection and imagination." Why are all these precious things, these special gifts, locked up and hidden away?

In Hablot K. ("Phiz") Browne's illustration for Amy's story of the Princess, Amy is leaning on her elbows, looking out the narrow window as the rays of the setting sun stream into the room. (Amy spends a lot of time looking out of windows, both at the Marshalsea and when she is abroad with her family.) You can just make out the wall with the spikes, and some chimneys off in the distance (Figure 3.2). As Amy looks "musingly down into the dark valley of the prison," she sees Pancks getting up to his usual mysterious tricks. She is saturated in the glow of the setting sun. "The sunset flush was so bright on Little Dorrit's face when she came thus to the end of her story," Dickens writes, "that she interposed her hand to shade it." (1.24) In another illustration, from an important chapter in Book 2, Amy is leaving the Marshalsea. Someone inside is holding open the door for her (Figure 3.3). The light from the prison streams out into the darkness. Amy's face is oddly featureless, like a doll's or a puppet's.

Dickens's verbal chiaroscuro throughout *Little Dorrit* is reflected in these illustrations. They seem to speak to each other. In one, beams of light come from *outside*, penetrating Amy's dark garret, reddening her face. In the other, the light pours from *inside* into the darkness of the street, and her face is turned away. In both, she stands in the stream of light. In one she is looking into the sun; in the other the light is behind her. In one she is inside; in the other

Figure 3.2 The Story of the Princess

she is outside, or on the threshold. In one, her love for Arthur is still inside her, it's her secret. In the other, when she visits Arthur at the Marshalsea, her love is on the outside, she has given it to him—for that faint form is Arthur standing at the prison door. The matching text for the second illustration is only two sentences: "Again tenderly wrapping her mantle about her, and taking her on his arm (though, but for her visit, he was almost too weak to walk), Arthur led Little Dorrit down-stairs. She was the last

Figure 3.3 The title page of *Little Dorrit*

visitor to pass out at the Lodge, and the gate jarred heavily and hopelessly upon her." (2.29) This illustration was later used as the title page of the novel. Yet it is very oblique and hard to interpret. Is it an image of fear or of hope? Does the woman step outside with the lightness of liberty, or with some trepidation into a dark, uncertain world? One scholar has remarked that Amy looks "as if she is bowed down with resignation."[27] I find that odd. To me, her little doll face looks almost joyful. What I see in these illustrations is a person who accepts life's dualities. Amy can stand in bright light and in dark shadows, something centers her. She remains quietly herself.

The chapter that includes the second illustration is called "A Plea in the Marshalsea," and it appeared in the last double number of *Little Dorrit*. Arthur has spent five feverish nights in the prison. On this, the sixth night, he wakes to the fragrance of a bouquet of flowers, and then sees Amy's form in the doorway, like an apparition: "Little Dorrit, a living presence, called him by his name." Amy and Maggy unpack their basket of provisions, she makes the room neat, and then sits beside Arthur and takes out her needle-case to make him a curtain for his window.

> To see the modest head again bent down over its task, and the nimble fingers busy at their old work...to be so consoled and comforted, and to believe that all the devotion of this great nature was turned to him in his adversity to pour out its inexhaustible wealth of goodness upon him, did not steady Clennam's trembling voice or hand, or strengthen him in his weakness. Yet it inspired him with an inward fortitude, that rose with his love. And how dearly he loved her now, what words can tell! (2.29)

As in so many scenes set in this room, the sun is going down, and the wall of the prison casts its ominous shadow. But now Dickens writes, "As they sat side by side in the shadow of the wall, the shadow fell like light upon him."(2.29) Slowly this shadow moves with the sun, until the sun disappears and one bright star shows in the night sky. It shines down on Amy.

Only the night before, Arthur learned of Amy's love for him. Now everything seems inverted. The shadow fell like light. The light touch Young John Chivery lays on Arthur's chest with the back of his hand feels like a violent blow. Arthur is like "a man who has been awakened from sleep." When he returns to his room, "The feeling of the blow was still so strong upon him," that "he sat down in the faded arm-chair, pressing his head between his hands, as if he had been stunned. Little Dorrit love him! More bewildering to him than his misery, far." (2.27) Her name sounds in his heart like an incantation. "Little Dorrit, Little Dorrit. Again, for hours. Always Little Dorrit!" The words are like a spell, a charm. Dickens finds a wonderful image for Arthur's emotional and psychological awakening. "Dear Little Dorrit. Looking back upon his own poor story, she was its vanishing-point. Every thing in its perspective led to her innocent figure." (2.27) Everything for Arthur is pulled into focus because of her love. "All those lights were extinguished," he had told Mr. Meagles. Not yet. Not quite.

When he first learns her story, Arthur thinks he understands Amy. But for a long time, he only sees her outline, that she grew up in a prison, that her father is a scamp and a sham: "He saw the devoted little creature with her worn shoes, in her common dress, in her jail-home; a slender child in body, a strong heroine in soul; and the light of her domestic story made all else dark to him." (1.32) Only much later, when William Dorrit is about to be released from prison, does he begin to see her complexity. Amy says it seems hard that her father should have to pay off all his debts, "that he should pay in life and money both." When Arthur begins to remonstrate, she says "Yes, I know I am wrong...don't think any worse of me; it has grown up with me here."

> The prison, which could spoil so many things, had tainted Little Dorrit's mind no more than this. Engendered as the confusion was, in compassion for the poor prisoner, her father, it was the first speck Clennam had ever seen, it was the last speck Clennam ever saw, of the prison atmosphere upon her.
>
> He thought this, and forbore to say another word. With the thought, her purity and goodness came before him in their brightest light. The little spot made them the more beautiful. (1.35)

Here is Murdoch's "loving attention," the capacity to see the taint, the speck of shame that clings to an individual as something inextricable from who she is, a necessary part of what makes her virtuous and lovable. Arthur does not realize he is in love with Amy, he hasn't given himself permission to love any woman yet, old man that he is—he renounced that dream when he let Minnie Meagles's rose petals drift down the river. But Arthur's respect for Amy, his restraint in correcting her misguided admiration for her father, is most loving. He does not remonstrate with her, not now or at any other time when William Dorrit behaves badly. His role is not to save her, but simply to see her. That little spot is what makes her nobility shine like the sun. Yes, Arthur loves Amy because he believes she is good, as Amy loves Arthur because she believes he is good. There is nothing wrong with that reasoning, in my opinion, we all need someone to admire morally. But the fact that he *sees* the little spot the prison has made grounds his love not in fantasy, as David first loved Dora, but in reality.

"I have thought of you—" Arthur says. He hesitates what to call her. Amy perceives it in an instant. "You have not spoken to me by my right name yet. You know what my right name always is with you."(2.29) Only once does Arthur call her Amy. She corrects him: "'Little Dorrit. Never any other name.' (It was she who whispered it.)" (2.34) Does she whisper it or does it whisper her? Where did Dickens find this name? Flora Finching says that Little Dorrit is "of all the strangest names I ever heard the strangest, like a place down in the country with a turnpike, or a favourite pony or a puppy or a bird or something from a seed-shop to be put in a garden or a flower-pot and come up speckled." (1.23) I love her for that little extemporization. And by the way, there's nothing wrong with Flora's heart, as Dickens plainly wants us to see, as there's nothing wrong with Young John's. And now may I confess how I adore this character? Young John may be only a turnkey, but he has the native delicacy of a gentleman. Young John knows love, and he knows what it is to try to heal a broken heart, for as he tells Arthur, "that doesn't justify throwing a person back upon himself after he has struggled and strived out of himself like a butterfly." (2.27) "My son has a 'art, and my son's 'art is in the right place," says Mr. Chivery. "Me and his mother knows where to find it, and we find it sitiwated correct." (2.27)

But the name. "Little—? Dorrit? That's the seamstress who was mentioned to me by a small tenant of mine?" Mr. Casby asks Arthur. "Yes, yes. Dorrit? That's the name. Ah, yes, yes! You call her Little Dorrit?" (1.13) Arthur has called her Little Dorrit since the night she and Maggy came to see him at his lodgings in Covent Garden, the night of her party, when she gets locked out. On that evening, he wants to call her "my child," but catches himself. It makes Amy uncomfortable.

> "I wanted a tender word, and could think of no other. As you just now gave yourself the name they give you at my mother's, and as that is the name by which I always think of you, let me call you Little Dorrit."
> "Thank you, sir, I should like it better than any name."
> "Little Dorrit." (1.14)

After that night, "Little Dorrit" is in almost every sentence he utters to her, for "the phrase had already begun, between these two, to stand for a hundred gentle phrases, according to the varying tone and connection in which it was used."(1.14) Little Dorrit. Always, Little Dorrit. Except to me she is always Amy. *Aimee* in French, from the Latin name *Amata*, derived from *amatus*. Beloved.

Who is Amy? I can't see her clearly, little speck on the horizon line, littlest star in the vast sky. "It was not easy to make out Little

Dorrit's face; she was so retiring, plied her needle in such removed corners." "But it seemed to be a pale transparent face, quick in expression, though not beautiful in feature, its soft hazel eyes excepted. A delicately bent head, a tiny form, a quick little pair of busy hands, and a shabby dress…were Little Dorrit as she sat at work." (1.5) She evokes my sculpture by Bourgeois, intent inside her glass circle, head bent, holding the burden of her family's evasions. Is it a burden of love and sacrifice, or is it a dangerous obsession? Is she safe in her corner? Today in the Church of Saint George the Martyr in Southwark, adjacent to the one remaining wall of the Marshalsea Prison, in the left panel of a stained-glass window behind the altar depicting Saint George with his sword, directly under his foot, in the corner, there is a small figure of a kneeling girl, hands in prayer, with a straw bonnet strung round her back. Amy. She wears a gold medallion around her neck with the letter "D" inscribed on it. The window was put in after the war, in 1951. I wonder what it looks like when the light streams in (Figure 3.4).

"It was a girl, surely, whom I saw near you," says Arthur, "—almost hidden in the dark corner?" Almost hidden. Not quite.

"This history must sometimes see with Little Dorrit's eyes."(1.14) A child born in a prison must have a special way of seeing, an exceptional sensitivity to insides and outsides. Amy has learned to apprehend the world "through a grating," in stripes and zig-zags of light and shade: "many light shapes did the strong iron weave itself into, many golden touches fell upon the rust…New zig-zags sprung into the cruel pattern sometimes, when she saw it through a burst of tears; but beautified or hardened still, always over it and under it and through it, she was fain to look in her solitude, seeing everything with that ineffaceable brand." (1.7, 1.24)

Figure 3.4 Little Dorrit window in the Church of Saint George the Martyr

What is Amy's relationship to the world? What exactly does she see? If I could begin to understand this question, I might discover why I care about *Little Dorrit*, pull together the past and present, the words, people, images that gather me in their orbits, and find some kind of meaning—at least a reason for writing, instead of this endless circling. I do identify with sad old Arthur, he's so underconfident. But Amy is the vanishing point. She may even be the most beautiful character in Dickens, worthy of a window in a church. Yet she is so vulnerable, so terribly violated. Does she see how awful her family is? "Worldly wise in hard and poor necessities, she was innocent in all things else. Innocent, in the mist through which she saw her father, and the prison, and the turbid living river that flowed through it and flowed on." (1.7) Through the ineffaceable brand and the mist, through the spikes and iron bars, through shadow and golden light, what does she see? The truth about people, or their masks and their lies? She loves her father. Does her love empower her or impede her? How much does she know?

Amy is the Child of the Marshalsea, youngest of three in the Dorrit family, born in the summer, in a stifling room covered with flies, her mother attended by two drunkards. When she is very little she forms an attachment to Bob the turnkey, her "godfather," and after her mother dies when she is eight she becomes her father's favorite, his sympathizer, shield, and footstool. Every family has its game, as Winnicott called it. The Dorrit game is that they are genteel and, through no fault of their own, they have taken a step down the ladder—temporarily, temporarily. Everyone has an assigned role: the "aristocratic brother," the "dainty" sister, the hapless uncle, and the patriarch, bearer of all their "forlorn gentility." (1.18, 1.20, 1.7) People outside the family are deployed, almost automatically, to keep this mythology intact. Young John Chivery, for instance, is made a peg "on which to air the miserably ragged old fiction of the family gentility." (1.18) Amy is another peg. In *The Drama of the Gifted Child*, Alice Miller writes about a certain kind of sensitive child: "His sensibility, his empathy, his intense and differentiated emotional responsiveness, and his unusually powerful 'antennae' seem to predestine him as a child to be used—if not misused—by people with intense narcissistic needs."[28] Amy's job in the family is to absorb everyone's emotions, to be used or misused by them for their own purposes. "She took the place of eldest of the three, in all things but precedence; was the head of the fallen family; and bore, in her own heart, its anxieties and shames." (1.7) This, however, cannot be admitted. So it "was the family custom to lay it down as family law, that [Amy] was a plain domestic little creature, without the great and sage experience of the rest. This family fiction was the family assertion of itself against her services. Not to make too much of them." (1.20)

Arthur doesn't like Amy to call the Marshalsea home. "But it is home! What else can I call home?" (1.22) There's nowhere else, as Arthur of all people must know. The youngest child in a family has to decipher how the little community she's found herself in is ordered, and she has to learn how to survive within it. "What her pitiful look saw, at that early time, in her father, in her sister, in her brother, in the jail; how much, or how little of the wretched truth it pleased God to make visible to her; lies hidden with many mysteries." (1.7) Dickens says she is "inspired," as a poet or a priest is, to do the right thing, to love the people in her life, to look out for them. As a child, Amy learns to say, "Excuse me sir, I was born here," and so acquires a dancing master for her sister. She sees that Tip will never amount to anything, so she asks Arthur not to bail him out. When her mother dies, she observes her father closely and "the protection that her wondering eyes had expressed towards him, became embodied in action, and the Child of the Marshalsea took upon herself a new relation towards the Father." "With a pitiful and plaintive look for everything, indeed, but with something in it for only him that was like protection…" (1.7) She knows that her family has a way of corrupting people. "But I am afraid," she admits to Arthur, "to leave him, I am afraid to leave any of them. When I am gone, they pervert—but they don't mean it—even Maggy." (1.22) She knows she's been tainted by the prison and by this family. She tells Arthur, "It was but the other day that my sister told me I had become so used to the prison that I had its tone and character. It must be so. I am sure it must be when I see these things." (1.22)

Yet there are things she cannot see and cannot admit, including her own collusion in the family fiction. Amy pleads with Arthur, "I hope you will not misunderstand my father. Don't judge him, sir, as you would judge others outside the gates. He has been there so long! I never saw him outside, but I can understand that he must have grown different in some things since." (1.9) "He only requires to be understood. I only ask for him that his life may be fairly remembered."(1.9) Does Amy see how atrocious he is? She knows her father has encouraged Young John's suit for his own selfish reasons—he likes receiving those cigars every Sunday, and there would be other perks if his daughter married the turnkey's son. "'It's impossible to forget,' turning his hands over and over and looking closely at them, 'that—hem!—that in such a life as mine, I am unfortunately dependent on these men for something every hour in the day,'" he reminds her. Amy cannot look at him, and she remains silent. It's impossible to believe. Earlier that evening she had been approached by Young John on the Iron Bridge. When he tells Amy her father told him where to find her, she turns her face from him and murmurs, "O father, father!" "Little Dorrit, with her hands to her averted face, and rocking herself where she stood as if she were in pain, murmured, 'O father, how can you! O dear, dear father, how can you, can you, do it!'" When she hears her father's insinuations, in this one instance, only this once in the entire novel, she is forced to plead for herself: "Only think of me, father, for one little moment!" (1.19)

> As she stood behind him, leaning over his chair so lovingly, he looked with downcast eyes at the fire. An uneasiness stole over him

that was like a touch of shame; and when he spoke, as he presently did, it was in an unconnected and embarrassed manner.

"I—hem!—I can't think, Amy, what has given Chivery offence. He is generally so—so very attentive and respectful. And to-night he was quite—quite short with me. Other people there too! Why, good Heaven! if I was to lose the support and recognition of Chivery and his brother officers, I might starve to death here." While he spoke, he was opening and shutting his hands like valves; so conscious all the time of that touch of shame, that he shrunk before his own knowledge of his meaning. (1.19)

"Opening and shutting his hands like valves." In this gesture we see how easily William can turn his feelings off and on, and the "touch of shame" it exposes—indeed, shame is the keynote in *Little Dorrit*, shame and guilt. William's conscience "shrinks" from his manipulation of his daughter. Yet he does it, and quite skillfully. As Amy silently prepares his meal, his agitation grows, until "in a burst of maudlin pity" he tells her how he used to be, how handsome, how respected before his years in the prison. In great distress, in shame, the Father of the Marshalsea "revealed his degenerate state to his affectionate child. No one else ever beheld him in the details of his humiliation." After making his daughter his witness, he transfers all responsibility for his condition to her: "She soothed him; asked him for his forgiveness if she had been, or seemed to have been, undutiful; told him, Heaven knows truly, that she could not honour him more if he were the favourite of Fortune and the whole world acknowledged him. When his tears were dried, and he sobbed in his weakness no longer, and was *free from that touch of shame*, and had recovered his usual bearing…" (1.19) Amy assumes the burden of his remorse, she frees him from himself, and restores her father to his role as martyr and benefactor. When he talks about his years in prison it is "with a catch in his breath that was not so much a sob as an irrepressible sound of self-approval, the momentary outburst of a noble consciousness. 'It is all I could do for my children—I have done it. Amy, my love, you are by far the best loved of the three; I have had you principally in my mind—whatever I have done for your sake, my dear child, I have done freely and without murmuring.'" (1.19) Her father's dependence on her and her protection of him have established a script, now unshakeable, in which she is the recipient of *his* guardianship and kindness, and *she* is the guilty party—when she walks with Old Nandy, when she refuses Young John, when she tells Arthur not to give him money, when she wears her old blue dress, when she fails to please Mrs. General, in all these acts she is branded as a misfit, the traitor to the family pact.

The relationship between Amy and her father is a disturbing portrait of emotional abuse. Dickens dramatizes this kind of love very accurately and very well. He doesn't need a psychological theory to explain it, for this is how people are, this is just what happens, the reasons are beyond justification. "Only the wisdom that holds the clue to all hearts and all mysteries," he writes, "can surely know to what extent a man, especially a man brought down as this man had been, can impose upon himself." After "bestowing his life of degradation as a sort of portion on the devoted child upon whom its miseries had fallen so heavily," William Dorrit lies down in majestic manner, with tears in his eyes. Amy "had no doubts, asked herself no question." At the end of this chapter, "in a burst of sorrow and compassion," she says. "No, no, I have never seen him in my life!" (1.19) She accepts it all.

One evening, when the family is living in luxury in Italy, William comes upon Amy and her uncle sitting together in an alcove. They seem close, happy. He experiences a pang of jealousy. It is as if

Frederick has taken his place. "Yet surely there was nothing to be jealous of in the old miserable poverty. Whence, then, the pang in his heart?" When Amy looks up at him with concern, "he feels the pain again, in his poor weak breast, so full of contradictions, vacillations, inconsistencies, the little peevish perplexities of this ignorant life, mists which the morning without a night only can clear away." He becomes petulant and frosty, self-defensively projecting his fears onto his brother. "I want no help," he says bitterly to Amy, "I am your father, not your infirm uncle!" Then he "checked himself, as abruptly as he had broken into this reply, and said, 'You have not kissed me, Amy.'" (2.19) The sudden swings from self-pity to anger are the reactions of someone suffering either from dementia or acute self-division. And it is on the very next evening, at Mrs. Merdle's grand dinner, that William Dorrit reverts tragically to the old self, to the Father of the Marshalsea. We see his humiliation (though Amy is not ashamed of him), and the adverse and intractable bond between father and daughter. Dickens writes nothing sadder than this chapter.

> Saving that he once asked 'if Tip had gone outside?' the remembrance of his two children not present seemed to have departed from him. But the child who had done so much for him and had been so poorly repaid, was never out of his mind. Not that he spared her, or was fearful of her being spent by watching and fatigue; he was not more troubled on that score than he had usually been. No; he loved her in his old way. They were in the jail again, and she tended him, and he had constant need of her, and could not turn without her; and he even told her, sometimes, that he was content to have undergone a great deal for her sake. As to her, she bent over his bed with her quiet face against his, and would have laid down her own life to restore him. (2.19)

This way of loving is permanently etched upon the hearts of these two human beings. She is the best loved child, she is his protector, he relies upon her for everything and bestows upon her all the gifts of his position. So different in age, in sex, in feeling, they are tied as parent and child by innumerable obligations and desires, by so many complicated interdependencies. "They were in the jail again," Dickens writes truthfully. They were home.

"When are you coming home?" The eternal question. I can hear my mother's voice, half-joking, a bit of self-parody for which I love her. She liked playing the guilt-inducing mother. But there was also in those words a plea for the past, a desire wrought by love. She wanted me there, I had to be part of the family group, my presence was required for whatever reason. Maybe she just missed me.

"If it's not one thing, it's your mother," our family always joked. We liked to tease Mom about her controlling personality. "Get off the eggs, Flo!" my uncle used to tell her. "It's always the mother's fault," my intellectual brother once blandly remarked—Joseph, who read everything Freud wrote, who asked my mother once about his toilet training, trying to get to the bottom of some mystery in himself. Did my parents know my brother was gay? When I was home for a visit in August 2017, five months after dad's death, my mother and I were talking about what kind of cancer Joseph died from, it spread so quickly we were never really sure. "All his stuff is in a box in the closet upstairs," she said. That night, I took the box into the bedroom I used, Joseph's old room, got into bed and went through the pathology reports. In a page about patient information there was a line heavily blacked out. I held the paper up to the light and could see the typed words: "Is gay, but not sexually active." Who drew that black marker across those words? Joseph? A doctor? My father or mother? Or was it someone else. I looked at that heavy black stripe with gigantic sorrow. Why did my gifted brother have to hide who he was, even as he was dying.

My mother was confident that she knew her children. She liked to proclaim, "I know my own children, I raised them!" Except she never had the faintest idea that after my sister Susan graduated from college, she left Cleveland—she left *the family*—and moved to another city not for a job, as I did, but so she could live her own life as gay woman. She did not come out to my parents until she was fifty years old, and they did not see it coming, not for miles. When I was with my mother in the hospital the month she died, she was still marveling that she never solved this piece of the family puzzle: "So *that's* why she had to leave Cleveland . . ." I am still not sure if my father ever understood. As far as I know, the subject of who my sister is, what she had to camouflage and conceal all her life, was never brought up again.

When I was sitting with Mom in the hospital at the end of July in 2019, sometimes a nurse who was checking on her would greet me and say, "This must be your daughter!" or "You look just like your mother." Mom couldn't see it. "Really?" she'd say, skeptically. "On no, I don't think so." As I get older, I see Mom in the mirror more and more. I've heard this happens as you age—I see my father's hooded Italian eyes in Susan, his nose and mouth in Tom. Just the other day my sister told me that in a Zoom recital she noticed that my hands on the piano keys looked exactly like Joseph's (and eerily I was playing music out of one of his old books, with pencil markings made by his piano teacher from high school). When I would tell Mom I could see her features in me, she'd say, in a tone I remember so well, "Oh poor you!" I loved her black eyes, truly black, although in the last month, I noticed they were lighter, more gray than black. When Patricia saw Mom's photograph on the funeral home's obituary page, she told me, "You look alike, same mouth, same nose." At the funeral a friend of my brother's told me I looked like Mom in some of the old photographs.

Mom and I were not alike in other ways though (when I told her that I thought, in some ways we were *very* alike, she'd scrunch her nose and shake her head). I wish I had her directness, her confidence, and the way she trusted in her own judgment. She didn't second guess herself the way I do. This meant Mom found it very difficult to apologize. She told me more than once, and this was when she was in her nineties, that she had no regrets about anything she'd done in her life. "Maybe that's wrong," she told me, "but that's how I feel." My mother liked lively debate, the family around her table, card games (she was quite competitive), and many people to feed. I cannot begin to count how many times in my life she hollered up the stairs for me to come down and join in some game or family conversation. Patricia pointed out that with my older siblings at school, I would have been with my mother almost constantly in the first five years of my life. Her imprint was deep, as was her authority (I have always been very obedient to authority figures). In therapy, I started to remember incidents over the years in which I felt wounded by something my mother had said—not on purpose, she was never mean, but she tended to minimize things I cared about or needed emotionally. I began to pay attention to the way my mother and I interacted. I noticed that she seemed impatient with me and that I was nervous around her, I could not think of things to say that might interest her. Perhaps she felt the same way. Mom tried to understand me, I know this.

But the more tentative way I approached the world jarred with her practicality. My emotionality, perhaps, made her uncomfortable (she never got depressed). I think this made me seem to her insufficient or incompetent. For example, she never gave me important tasks when she was putting on a big dinner. In what became a ludicrous family joke, I was the only one in the extended family who was not allowed to drive the Buick because, for some reason, my mother thought I couldn't handle it. On my visits home, I had to pay for a rental car even though a perfectly good vehicle was sitting in the garage. A few years ago at a family gathering with my do-it-yourself relatives, my mother loudly announced, "Annette can't do anything—except—." The room waited expectantly. She didn't finish the sentence. The word on the tip of her tongue, of course, was "read."

As I said earlier in this book, I always felt loved. But Patricia wondered if I was really seen. When I came home, whatever I had accomplished in my career, whatever I had experienced recently in my personal life, got swallowed up in the group. I am not saying I was ignored, or that my parents were not proud of me. But at the lively family table, I often felt drowned out, overwhelmed. I could not compete. This is the only way I can think of to describe it, that I was outplayed. What delighted or amused my mother, cooking, politics, tv, sports, gossip about people—that wasn't where I lived, mentally or emotionally, and it was terrible to try to fake it. Unlike my smart, talkative sister, I did not watch television or keep up with political debates, and unlike my wonderfully likable brother I could not tell funny stories about the characters I met at work. I was a divided person the moment I set foot in the house, trying to be compliant and to please her, while at the same time subconsciously protecting my own inner being, Winnicott's "true self." I suffered profuse private meltdowns when I went home, not now and then, but consistently, for more than two decades. I could not understand what was the matter with me. My siblings were funny and witty, my parents dependable and ever giving. *I love my family*, I'd insist to Patricia. *I know you do*, she would say. *Tell me about these meltdowns.*

One Christmas, when Dad was in decline and nerves were frayed, I wanted to help, I had ideas I thought we could talk about. My take on things, though, was summarily rejected, my feelings pushed away. When would I be taken seriously? In an astonishing outburst, my mother turned to me and yelled, "When you prove yourself, Annette! When you finally prove yourself!" This took my breath away. Did she really say those words? In the worry and stress of that moment, she had finally, angrily, told the truth. I was 56 years old, and there it was. I had not proven myself. It resonated with so much Patricia and I had been talking about, I went to my bedroom literally shaking. For I finally understood. I never would prove myself to my mother, no matter what I did, so I didn't have to try any more. It felt as though someone had opened the door of a prison.

In one of my last sessions with Patricia, about four months after my mother's death, I was saying something about what a great woman Mom was. Patricia put down her pen, folded her hands and looked at me with unutterable gentleness. "From the very first day I met you, you have defended her," she said. "Did you know that?" I didn't know, how could I know? It has taken my whole life to see that I could love someone very much and also be angry at them, that I could be dutiful to my parents and also assert my own will. (And yes, it *hurt* me that my mother did not disguise from me her disapproval of Charles.) And for goodness' sake, I can retreat from the group, I can go into my room, I can read a book, it is not an act of betrayal. After a social occasion, Marion Milner writes how she needs to be alone to digest the experience, to make time "for the flood of another personality to subside."[29] May Sarton records that "being with people or even with one beloved person for any length of time without solitude" makes her lose her "center," she feels "dispersed, scattered to pieces."[30] When I came across these authors, I felt such recognition and relief. I was not an aberration; I was just different from my mother—as Patricia was trying to get me to see. Along with a few other things.

That August when I went through my brother's medical records, I also helped Mom go through my father's closet and sort out his clothes for Goodwill. As we bagged and boxed his shirts, shoes, ties, handkerchiefs, she recalled their life together. She mentioned what a catch he was, how easy-going. "Your father, he never denied me anything," she said. We sat on the bed and went through his things and remembered him. Just over two years later, on a damp, cold day in November, I was going through her things, aprons, scarves, gloves, underclothes. I wasn't looking for anything, I wasn't remembering anything, I was just sorting, one box for things to throw out, one box for things I wanted. Photographs, linens, knick-knacks. But I didn't really want any of it, my heart wasn't in it. I would take the boxes back to my house in Virginia, and then what would I do with them? Put them in the attic and forget. Until one day something happens or doesn't happen, something snags at a question or a memory, and I feel the need to remember.

At the end of *Little Dorrit*, the good people do not retreat into domesticity or form an exclusive little circle, as they do at the end of *Oliver Twist*, *Dombey and Son*, *David Copperfield*, *Bleak House*. There are no more endings like that in any of Dickens's novels after *Little Dorrit*. Dickens knew the world and its crimes can no longer be escaped from or hidden from view. Society is corrupt, but this is the world Amy and Arthur must act in. And so after they sign the marriage registry, "Little Dorrit and her husband" (note the order) walk out of the Church of Saint George the Martyr alone. "They paused for a moment on the steps of the portico, looking at the fresh perspective of the street in the autumn morning sun's bright rays, and then went down."

> Went down into a modest life of usefulness and happiness. Went down to give a mother's care, in the fulness of time, to Fanny's neglected children no less than to their own, and to leave that lady going into Society for ever and a day. Went down to give a tender nurse and friend to Tip for some few years, who was never vexed by the great exactions he made of her in return for the riches he might have given her if he had ever had them, and who lovingly closed his eyes upon the Marshalsea and all its blighted fruits. They went quietly down into the roaring streets, inseparable and blessed; and as they passed along in sunshine and shade, the noisy and the eager, and the arrogant and the froward and the vain, fretted and chafed, and made their usual uproar. (2.34)

This is what Dickens can do with poetic understatement. "Very quiet conclusion," he wrote in his Working Notes to the novel. And I confess when I get to the end of Little Dorrit sometimes there are tears in my eyes. In sunshine and in shade, the world continues as usual to run in mad circles, people rush about on their "errands of mercy or errands of sin."[31] Somehow, by a miracle, Arthur and Amy have not succumbed to the madness. They go on and they do what they can, for Fanny's children, for poor Tip, and for their own children. They have come through. As Patricia said to me once, "All you have to do is survive."

As a child, Amy had "no earthly friend to help her, or so much as to see her," she was "born and bred in a social condition, false even with a reference to the falsest condition outside the walls; drinking from infancy of a well whose waters had their own peculiar stain, their own unwholesome and unnatural taste…" (1.7) The prison contaminates. But as Dickens maintains, the whole society is tainted: the prison is "false even with a reference to the falsest condition outside the wall." It is just a matter of degree.

The stain is of the world. It is of the western world, especially. The former Green Party councilor who spray-painted "Dickens Racist" on the wall of the Dickens House in Broadstairs, Kent in June 2020 may feel strongly that reading Dickens will not help to advance movements for racial equality that are convulsing the world today. Dickens, for all his hatred of tyranny, was the inheritor of pernicious racialized ideologies.[32] In January 2021, The Dickens Society published an anti-racist statement promising to examine "the manifold ways in which Dickens's life and career must be considered in light of their implicit dependence upon the structures of racism that make movements such as Black Lives Matter necessary in the twenty-first century."[33] Other manifestos confronting the inherent racism in Victorian studies have also recently appeared. No doubt this is all for the best.

We can take an unforgivably long time to see the beam in our own eye. It is hard to trace how any one person's feelings and ideas evolve, how one mind slowly opens. A manifesto or social justice movement may revolutionize someone. Maybe a character in a novel or a movie can shed a little light, or being helped by a stranger, or witnessing a bit of rudeness in the checkout line. Books are not everything, opinions are not everything. Statistics cannot show when a person has changed, or what effort has been made. Recall Murdoch's example of M and D. Just because M doesn't act on a decision does not mean she has not made considerable moral progress at a private level; her "inner acts" form part of her "continuous fabric of being." As Murdoch trenchantly points out, "Innumerable novels contain accounts of what such struggles are like."[34] Very many people in the west want to recognize who we have been and what we have done. The philosopher Richard Rorty argues that the fact that western culture has become "conscious of its capacity for murderous intolerance" and is much more wary of its predilections is a positive development, a potentially productive collective guilt. Some feelings are too hard to live with, and eventually we will have to deal with them. Our sorrow, self-hatred, and tremendous remorse may signal a desire to do better than our ancestors.[35]

There is a need for public acknowledgement of the past, and personally I think some kind of reparation has to be made. But for change to happen, the past has to be felt by people, it has to haunt and hurt us as individuals, the way Arthur is haunted by the sources of his family's money, the way Amy is hurt by her contact with the prison. And both of these characters are greatly conflicted, because what hurts them is also where they live, it is their history, their family, their home. I suppose this is where I started, with the Trump supporters and the Jungian podcasts, and with those complicated emotions, pride and shame. Amy is not ashamed of being born in the Marshalsea, that wasn't her choice or her fault. But she feels tainted by it just the same, as Arthur does when he is locked up there. Why wouldn't they? Debtors' prisons were a degrading and humiliating system. They were finally abolished in 1869, the year before Dickens died. "Thirty years ago there stood, a few doors short of the church of Saint George, in the borough of Southwark, on the left-hand side of the way going southward, the Marshalsea Prison," Dickens writes. "It had stood there many years before, and it remained there some years afterwards; but it is gone now, and the world is none the worse without it." (1.6) After he finished *Little Dorrit*, Dickens went to Southwark to look at what remained of the Marshalsea, to "stand among the crowding ghosts of many miserable years." For Dickens, they were private ghosts, his father and mother, brother and sister, and most of all his child self. Perhaps writing *Little Dorrit* was a way to lay them. But ghosts are restive and unruly. They can walk across oceans, and even centuries, to do their haunting.

When I moved to this community in central Virginia in 1991, the county jail was a red brick building near the courthouse in the center of downtown. Built in 1895, it was accommodated with living quarters in front for the sheriff and his family and had about 70 cells. It was remodeled in 1934, and in the 1960s 50 more cells were added. Some of them faced the street. I remember that when I walked down South Liberty Street, I could see some of the inmates looking out of the windows. And they could see me. It was an unsettling and depressing experience, and every time I took that route, I felt guilty and ashamed. Just six months later the old jail was demolished, along with other historic structures, to make way for a parking lot and a larger complex, grandly called the Rockingham-Harrisonburg Judicial Center, with space for 350 inmates and the sheriff's office. Now, after 20 years, the county wants to demolish another historic building for a projected expansion of the Judicial Center. The jail is filled to capacity.

The other day, I walked all around the jail complex. I looked up to the top floors, where I thought the prison cells might be. There are some rectangular slits, just wide enough, perhaps for someone inside to see a small patch of sky, a ray of sun or a shadow passing over a cloud. But other than that, there are no windows.

4

BUT FOR YOU, DEAR STRANGER

Dickens's first concern in all his fiction is with people's feelings and their imaginations. Everything else—the social criticism, the satire, the comedy—flows from that spring. How does a person begin to imagine, to enter vividly into the life he or she has been given, and into the lives of others? How does someone change, how do they love, give their trust, look forward to the future? These questions find their way into *Oliver Twist*, *David Copperfield*, and *Little Dorrit*. They also meaningfully inform the last novel I would like to think about in this short concluding chapter.

In *A Tale of Two Cities*, the exhibition of human suffering on a large scale is crucial to the execution of justice. Dickens's powerful description of the starving peasants in "The Wine-Shop" chapter make this clear: "The mill which had worked them down, was the mill that grinds young people old; the children had ancient faces and grave voices; and upon them, and upon the grown faces, and ploughed into every furrow of age and coming up afresh, was the sign, Hunger."[1] Reading the sign of misery is the beginning of sympathy. All of Dickens's novels insist upon the moral imperative of simply opening your eyes to the world around you. *A Christmas Carol*, for example, is all about the need to get out of your solitary oyster shell and notice that other people have problems, too. Scrooge at first resists the revelations of the Spirit of Christmas Past:

> "Spirit!" said Scrooge, "show me no more! Conduct me home. Why do you delight to torture me?"
> "One shadow more!" exclaimed the Ghost.
> "No more!" cried Scrooge. "No more. I don't wish to see it. Show me no more!"
> But the relentless Ghost pinioned him in both his arms, and forced him to observe what happened next.[2]

Richard Rorty has remarked, "Dickens did not want anybody to be transformed, except in one respect: he wanted them to notice and understand the people they passed on the street."[3] This is absolutely right. But as Scrooge's transformation teaches us, *noticing* and *understanding* can be very different things.

People are often incomprehensible to one another. The task of moral perception can feel like lumbering through darkness, feeling blindly for a light. And indeed, the inner lives of strangers and the strangeness of the self are among Dickens's persistent preoccupations in *A Tale of Two Cities*. The chapter called "Night Shadows" begins with a long meditation on this phenomenon: "A wonderful fact to reflect upon, that every human creature is constituted to be that profound secret and mystery to every other." Dickens calls the passengers in the mail-coach from Dover, evocatively, "three fellow-inscrutables." (1.3) Doctor Manette confesses to Charles Darnay, "mysteries arise out of close love, as well as out of wide division; in the former case, they are subtle and delicate, and difficult to penetrate. My daughter Lucie is, in this one respect, such a mystery to me." (2.10) It is not simply that people are strangers to one another. They are *mysteries*, fatally barred from what Yeats has called "the labyrinth of another's being."[4] They are even strangers to themselves, capable of unintended thoughts and perversities. "In seasons of pestilence, some of us will have a secret attraction to the disease—a terrible passing inclination to die of it," Dickens writes. "And all of us have like wonders hidden in our breasts, only needing circumstances to evoke them." (3.6) Circumstances such as a pandemic, or a violent social revolution. Or the look of anguish on the face of someone you love.

Sydney Carton, the hero of *A Tale of Two Cities*, tells Lucie Manette, that he cannot comprehend "the mystery of my own wretched heart." (2.13) He is one of my favorite characters in Dickens, my secret heart throb. Carton knows that he should change, he knows he could be a better man, but something inside him prevents him from doing anything about it. Carton's cynicism—"I care for no man on earth, and no man on earth cares for me"—masks his hurt and his unrelieved loneliness. (1.4) He is a man of strong emotion and innate decency, someone who is capable, as the story reveals, of almost unfathomable self-sacrifice. Carton *knows* that his life could be happier and that he could be a better person, but he's petrified by some wound in his past. "I am like one who died young," he tells Lucie. "All my life might have been." (2.13) His demeanor is insolent, his temperament moody and vacillating. Stryver calls him "the old seesaw Sydney. Up one minute and down the next; now in spirits and now in despondency." (2.5) Why is Carton so hopeless, so self-abandoned? We do not get much of a backstory. But Dickens was clearly drawn to this character. In a letter from 1859, he confessed, "I must say that I like my Carton. And I have a faint idea sometimes, that if I had acted him, I could have done something with his life and death."[5] In fact,

Dickens got the idea for Carton from the character of Richard Wardour, the self-sacrificing explorer in Wilkie Collins's play, *The Frozen Deep*. In amateur performances of the play, Dickens acted the part of Wardour with passionate concentration. I think he must have understood Carton's psychology intimately. I understand him, too, and my heart breaks for this character.

> Waste forces within him, and a desert all around, this man stood still on his way across a silent terrace, and saw for a moment, lying in the wilderness before him, a mirage of honourable ambition, self-denial, and perseverance. In the fair city of this vision, there were airy galleries from which the loves and graces looked upon him, gardens in which the fruits of life hung ripening, waters of Hope that sparkled in his sight. A moment, and it was gone. Climbing to a high chamber in a well of houses, he threw himself down in his clothes on a neglected bed, and its pillow was wet with wasted tears.
>
> Sadly, sadly, the sun rose; it rose upon no sadder sight than the man of good abilities and good emotions, incapable of their directed exercise, incapable of his own help and his own happiness, sensible of the blight on him, and resigning himself to let it eat him away. (2.5)

A grown man pities himself, cries into his pillow. Why has he wasted his life? Why is he so immobilized? Briefly, he is shown a *mirage* of another possible life. The waters of Hope sparkle before him. Then the picture vanishes.

Sydney Carton is always acting a part. Drunken and derisive, aloof and misanthropic, he is watchful, wary, and intuitive—he can tell if someone is a spy, if a man can be trusted or not. That is the person most people see, and they assume the pose is the man himself. We all play our roles. But to get through life, you have to have someone with whom you lower the mask, even if it's just once. "One confiding relationship, meaning a relationship where one is invited to speak one's heart and mind freely, offers the best protection against most forms of psychological trouble," writes Carol Gilligan.[6] Sydney Carton opens up to only one person in his entire life. Lucie Manette seems so perfect, so out of his league, so much above him. She inspires him with a dream of being better, and so he makes her his confidante:

> "I wish you to know that you have been the last dream of my soul. In my degradation I have not been so degraded but that the sight of you with your father, and of this home made such a home by you, has stirred old shadows that I thought had died out of me. Since I knew you, I have been troubled by a remorse that I thought would never reproach me again, and have heard whispers from old voices impelling me upward, that I thought were silent for ever. I have had unformed ideas of striving afresh, beginning anew, shaking off sloth and sensuality, and fighting out the abandoned fight. A dream, all a dream, that ends in nothing, and leaves the sleeper where he lay down, but I wish you to know that you inspired it."
> "Will nothing of it remain? O Mr. Carton, think again! Try again!"
> "No, Miss Manette; all through it, I have known myself to be quite undeserving. And yet I have had the weakness, and have still the weakness, to wish you to know with what a sudden mastery you kindled me, heap of ashes that I am, into fire—a fire, however, inseparable in its nature from myself, quickening nothing, lighting nothing, doing no service, idly burning away." (2.13)

This is a very serious confession, and though he calls his idealism a weakness (as Nancy does), opening up this way, trusting that Lucie will hear and understand him, is perhaps the second bravest thing Carton does in his life.

Everyone has a need to be known, "to have one's existence validated, to be affirmed in our very being, simply by being seen."[7] Think of Miss Wade's bitter record of her perceived abuse, which she thrusts upon Arthur Clennam, or Amy Dorrit's letters to him from Italy, her veiled confessions of love. While he was alive, Dickens did not tell anyone, not even his wife, about the humiliation he experienced as a child. But he wrote those memories down for someone to read some day, and bequeathed them to his closest friend, John Forster. The need to share who we are is a spiritual need, "a longing as deep as any that we have," as Jane Tompkins asserts. "In some circumstances, our emotional survival depends on our having a witness who will listen to us; it is all that we need, and without it, we cannot survive."[8] This is one reason people write, even guarded introverts like me. If life has taught me anything, it is that the need for self-expression is very great in people— look at social media and what the Internet has wrought. Look at this book on Dickens. There are thousands and thousands of people who want to tell complete strangers how life feels for them. They want to be noticed, yes. But they must hope, too, that in being noticed, they will also be understood.

Sydney Carton throws up many defenses against those lurking feelings of regret he confesses to Lucie, the desire deep within him to be a better man. He thinks he should succumb, that it is too late for him to change course (Nancy's words also). He has given in to addiction, to a perverse incapacity to act, to moral ennui: "the cloud of caring for nothing, which overshadowed him with such a fatal darkness, was very rarely pierced by the light within him." (2.13) But Carton still *has* a light within him. It is only misdirected. Lucie Manette sees it, and her "sweet compassion" brings it out. Lucie doesn't give up on Carton like everyone else does. She has faith, she is rooting for him.

I like to think of Sydney Carton as one of William James's twice-born souls: "There are persons whose existence is little more than a series of zigzags, as now one tendency and now another gets the upper hand. Their spirit wars with their flesh, they wish for incompatibles, wayward impulses interrupt their most deliberate plans, and their lives are one long drama of repentance and of effort to repair misdemeanors and mistakes."[9] Dickens writes often about people who strive and fail, or who drag on with disappointed lives. I am always struck by how many unhappy characters in Dickens's novels really do not know if they will be able to change or not. In Dickens, changing often means returning to a more spontaneous, child-like self, to become less worldly, less hard. It's good to remember that Scrooge, for instance, was not born angry at the world. In Stave Two, when the Spirit takes him back to his childhood, we see he was an imaginative and lonely boy, his mind delightedly swept away by tales of Ali Baba and Robinson Crusoe's parrot. He *weeps* when he sees who he once was. Scrooge lost his innocent spontaneity because he needed to acquire other qualities—energy, practicality, push—in order to make it. He became part of the new world order, ambitious to avoid the Hell of the English.[10] He can't be blamed, really. Young Scrooge is right when he complains, "This is the even-handed dealing of the world! There is nothing on which it is so hard as poverty; and there is nothing it professes to condemn with such severity as the pursuit of wealth!"[11] So a sensitive child turns hard, wards off feeling, builds a wall of money. But the time comes, usually in middle age, when the neglected psyche summons its ghosts.

I find it disquieting that in Dickens's novels, so many people's sufferings originate in loving someone. Mr. Dombey's love for his dead child, Mr. Wickfield's love for his dead wife, Miss Havisham's love for the man who jilted her, Mrs. Steerforth's love for her wayward son, even Mrs. Clennam's possessive love for her husband, justified by her righteousness. These are not people who just cannot get over losing someone or who have had their hearts broken. The cases are extreme. It is as though they want to get back at life for hurting them so much, to get revenge for having exposed themselves to love, and so their lives are ordered around a dangerous obsession. Gilligan describes people she met through her research who "know in some sense where they have sealed off love, the deals they have made and the compromises struck, always for good reason but often at an enormous cost. The awareness of complicity is so shameful that it often seems easier to justify it than experience and question what has been sacrificed."[12] But this is not what happens to Sydney Carton. Love does not distort his vision, but instead opens his eyes completely to a new life. His conversion is similar to what James describes in "A Certain Blindness in Human Beings":

> Only in some pitiful dreamer, some philosopher, poet, or romancer, or when the common practical man becomes a lover, does the hard externality give way, and a gleam of insight into . . . the vast world of inner life beyond us, so different from that of outer seeming, illuminate our mind. Then the whole scheme of our customary values gets confounded, then our self is riven and its narrow interests fly to pieces, then a new centre and a new perspective must be found.[13]

At the end of *A Tale of Two Cities*, when we hear Carton's posthumous voice looking into the future, we know that the light within him has opened the door to his redemption, to that vast world of his own moral potential. "They said of him, about the city that night, that it was the peacefullest man's face ever beheld there. Many added that he looked sublime and prophetic." (3.15) And he is prophetic. Now, after death, Carton sees with utter clarity a mirage that does *not* vanish into thin air. It becomes true. Carton's noble act preserves the futures of Lucie, Charles, their children, and their children's children.

> "I see the lives for which I lay down my life, peaceful, useful, pros-
> perous and
> happy, in that England which I shall see no more. I see Her with a
> child upon her
> bosom, who bears my name....
> "I see that child who lay upon her bosom and who bore my
> name, a man winning his way up in that path of life which once was
> mine. I see him winning it so well, that my name is made illustrious
> there by the light of his. I see the blots I threw upon it, faded away.
> I see him, fore-most of just judges and honoured men, bringing a
> boy of my name, with a forehead that I know and golden hair, to
> this place—then fair to look upon, with not a trace of this day's
> disfigurement—and I hear him tell the child my story, with a tender
> and a faltering voice.
> "It is a far, far better thing that I do, than I have ever done; it is a
> far, far better rest that I go to than I have ever known." (3.15)

I think the last 487 words of *A Tale of Two Cities* are just sublime.

Early in my teaching career, I once asked a class what they thought of this ending. Sydney Carton goes to the guillotine to save the life of his friend Charles Darnay, husband of Lucie Manette, the woman both men love. Darnay and Carton are simi-lar in appearance. Carton arranges to exchange places with Darnay in prison, so that he will die on the guillotine instead of Darnay. Carton sacrifices his life so that Lucie will have a future with the man she loves, the father of her child. And how typical of Dickens's art to introduce the character of the poor seamstress in the last chapters. She is number Twenty-Two, sentenced to death for nothing, for some made-up plot against the Republic. The compas-sion Lucie Manette has offered to Carton he now extends to this stranger. "As the last thing on earth that his heart was to warm and soften to, it warmed and softened to this pitiable girl." (3.13) In the moments before their execution, Carton descends from the tumbril "and the seamstress is lifted out next after him. He has not relinquished her patient hand in getting out, but still holds it as he promised. He gently places her with her back to the crashing engine that constantly whirrs up and falls, and she looks into his face and thanks him." (3.15)

> "But for you, dear stranger, I should not be so composed, for I am naturally a poor little thing, faint of heart; nor should I have been able to raise my thoughts to Him who was put to death, that we might have hope and comfort here to-day. I think you were sent to me by Heaven."
>
> "Or you to me," says Sydney Carton. "Keep your eyes upon me, dear child, and mind no other object."(3.15)

At the last extremity, the very last, Carton and the seamstress find strength in one another. Their clasped hands and fixed gaze are a human bond of compassion, given to them by God.

But why does Dickens need to bring in the poor seamstress at the climax of the novel? I think she is important because, in offering his protection to this terrified girl, we are able to see that Carton's spiritual transformation is complete, it is real. He does not die loving Lucie Manette, or not only loving Lucie. He dies loving a stranger. Carton has always been good at reading other people's motives and psychology. This is what makes him a sharp lawyer, Stryver's jackal. But now he exerts this ability to a much nobler end. Carton comprehends the girl's misery and turns his full moral attention on her. Even as he faces his own death, his first commitment is to help the poor seamstress get through this ordeal. Among all the atrocities Dickens dwells on in *A Tale of Two*

Cities, sometimes with great relish (as in the chapter called "The Grindstone"), this act of human recognition stands in huge moral relief. This is the moment of Carton's victory over himself, and his fullest offering of himself to another. But for you, dear stranger.

There is even something more. Carton has always pretended he didn't care about anything, that nothing mattered. Now, that capacity to minimize things serves both him and the seamstress. He sees with utter calm that his death is a small thing and perceives how transient his life is. Other people will follow, other footsteps will echo through the centuries after Sydney Carton's story is finished. Even the violent upheaval of France is just one moment on a prodigious human timeline, marked by the Woodman, Fate and the Farmer, Death, each evoked poetically by Dickens in the first chapter of *A Tale of Two Cities.*

Peter Brooks, in his classic study, describes melodrama as a sense-making enterprise. Melodrama represents a small hope that there is some kind of order and meaning in the way events unfold. If most of the time we submit to the necessity of repression, says Brooks, "at other times we feel the need for a melodramatized reality, both within and without ourselves." We need to feel we're part of a marvelous story, something that is unfolding outside of our line of vision, reaching into future generations, as in Sydney's posthumous prophecy. Far-fetched tales that pitch good against evil, says Brooks, are a "constant promise that life is truly inhabited by primal, intense, polarized forces—forces primal and intense because they are polarized—that can be made manifest."[14]

The 1935 film version of *A Tale of Two Cities,* directed by Jack Conway and starring Ronald Colman (another heart throb) is melodrama at its finest and always bring me to the verge of tears. I once watched the film in an auditorium with a group of Dickens scholars and was privately appalled at the utter erosion of my critical distance. I was gripped in some subliminal way that made me feel defenseless, especially at the scene with the seamstress (played by Isabel Jewell). The young woman has faced her destiny. Now Carton's turn has come. He waits on the stage of the guillotine, the mob roars in the background, the drums roll, and the camera moves up to the top of the apparatus as the ax is about to fall. And it does fall, but the camera does not follow its descent. Our gaze continues to drift up, over Paris, into the clouds, and as the noise below fades out, we hear Carton's famous final words, in that exquisite Ronald Colman voice, from somewhere in the heavens. I watched the film again recently, and I'm still enthralled and chilled by that ending. It perfectly captures the fading away of consciousness implied in Dickens's description: "The murmuring of many voices, the upturning of many faces, the pressing on of many footsteps in the outskirts of the crowd, so that it swells forward in a mass, like one great heave of water, all flashes away. Twenty-Three." (3.15) Twenty-Three is Sydney Carton. And then a pause, a white space on the page, and the last 487 words.

For all its over-the-topness, something about *A Tale of Two Cities* hits a nerve with me. Maybe I just love a good melodrama. But that feels dismissive, and it doesn't do justice to the sublimity of Dickens's vision. For Sydney Carton's act is one of extreme renunciation. It is a Christ-like act: "Greater love hath no man than this, that a man lay down his life for his friends."[15] In the film, when the seamstress asks Carton why he is taking Darnay's place he replies, simply, "He is my friend." How could anyone not be pulled in, just a little, by the suspense and poetry and moral beauty of this story?

But back to my class.

"No way," said Michael. Nineteen years old, some kind of business major, if I remember (though that could just be my bias). I sensed a teaching moment.

"No way, what?" I asked, cautiously.

"No way would a guy not take advantage of that situation to get the woman," he said. "He's going to console her and everything, you know, when the other guy is dead? So no way." He leaned back in his seat. "No guy would do that."

I was still a young teacher, this may even have been my first class on Dickens. I was simply *shocked* by this response to *A Tale of Two Cities*, a book that, in my mind, throbs with nobility. I looked swiftly around the room for dissenters and sensed complete neutrality on the question of Carton's offer to Lucie "to give his life, to keep a life you love beside you!" I was trying to get them to think about what Carton's death could mean symbolically, as an image of human aspiration, an act of selfless transcendence,—but what if they didn't get any of this in reading Dickens? What if they didn't get this about reading literature?

"No way," said Michael again. He looked very sure of himself.

I paused for a long moment, completely at a loss. And then without logic or premeditation I uttered the only words that would come to my astonished mind and I will never take them back.

"But isn't it a beautiful idea?"

ENDNOTES

Chapter 1

1. Dorianne Laux, "For the Sake of Strangers," *What We Carry* (Boa Editions, 1994), 23.
2. Anton Chekhov, *Fifty-Two Stories*, trans. Richard Pevear and Larissa Volokhonsky (Vintage Classics, 2021), 54. Ellipses in original.
3. Thornton Wilder, *Our Town* (Harper Perennial, 2003), 108.
4. The Victorian Web notes the illustration is James Mahoney's, from the Household Edition of *Oliver Twist* (1871).
5. Charles Dickens, *Oliver Twist* (1846), ed. Fred Kaplan (W. W. Norton, 1993), 61–62. For the convenience of readers using other editions, subsequent citations will be indicated parenthetically by chapter number.
6. Ali Smith, *Artful* (Penguin, 2014), 94.
7. Bertolt Brecht, *The Threepenny Opera*.
8. Henry James, *A Small Boy and Others* (Gibson Square Books, 2001), 61, 62.
9. Graham Greene, "The Young Dickens," *The Lost Childhood and Other Essays* (Viking, 1951), 51.
10. James, 63.
11. Marc Napolitano, *Oliver! A Dickensian Musical* (Oxford University Press, 2014), 44.
12. *Oliver!*, directed by Carol Reed (1968; Shepperton Studios, UK), Amazon Prime Video.
13. Napolitano, 187. In Dickens's novel, Fagin mixes Oliver "a glass of hot gin-and-water," and "Immediately afterwards he felt himself gently lifted on to one of the sacks; and then he sunk into a deep sleep."
14. Napolitano, 135.
15. Lionel Bart, "Be Back Soon," *Oliver!*, directed by Carol Reed (1968; Shepperton Studios, UK), Amazon Prime Video.
16. Napolitano, 65, 135, 65.
17. Napolitano, 30.
18. Napolitano, 31.

19. *The Guardian*, April 4, 1999.
20. Charles Dickens, *Bleak House*, Ch. 11.
21. John Bayley, "*Oliver Twist*: 'Things as They Really Are,'" *Dickens and the Twentieth Century*, eds. John Gross and Gabriel Pearson (Routledge, 1962), 54.
22. Greene, 56–57.
23. Isaac Chotiner, "Inside a Texas Building Where the Government Is Holding Immigrant Children," *The New Yorker*, June 22, 2019.
24. Bert G. Hornback, "Frustration and Resolution in *David Copperfield*," *Studies in English Literature, 1500–1900* 8.4 (Autumn 1968), 653.
25. Garry Wills, "Love in the Lower Depths," *The New York Review of Books* (October 26, 1989), 66–67.
26. From the Scottish ballad "Edward, Edward," by Anonymous.
27. From "September 1, 1939," by W. H. Auden.
28. From "Ode: Intimations of Immortality," by William Wordsworth.
29. John Forster, *The Life of Charles Dickens*, Vol. I, Ch. XIII; David Chandler, "Dickens on Wordsworth: *Nicholas Nickleby* and the Copyright Question," *English Language Notes* 41.1 (2003), 62–69.
30. Steven Marcus, *Dickens from Pickwick to Dombey* (W. W. Norton, 1963), 374.
31. Greene, 56.
32. Isaac Chotiner, "Inside a Texas Building Where the Government Is Holding Immigrant Children," *The New Yorker*, June 22, 2019.
33. Lisel Mueller, "Missing the Dead," *Alive Together: New and Selected Poems* (Louisiana State University Press, 1996), 197. I read this poem at my mother's funeral service.

Chapter 2

1. The Coodles, Doodles, etc. are from *Bleak House* (1852–53).
2. Charles Dickens, *David Copperfield*, ed. Jerome H. Buckley (W. W. Norton, 1990), 54. For the convenience of readers using other editions, subsequent citations will be indicated parenthetically by chapter number.
3. George Orwell, "Charles Dickens," *George Orwell: A Selection of Essays* (Harvest, 1946; 1980), 91.
4. Wolfgang Iser, "The Reading Process: A Phenomenological Approach," *New Literary History* 3.2 (1972), 283–84.
5. Gaston Bachelard, *The Poetics of Space*, trans. Maria Jolas (Penguin, 1964; 2014), 11.
6. Virginia Woolf, "David Copperfield," *The Moment and Other Essays* (Harcourt Brace, 1947; 1967), 78. My italics.

7. Virginia Woolf, "How Should One Read a Book?", *The Second Common Reader*, ed. Andrew McNeillie (Harcourt Brace Jovanovich, 1932; 1986), 260–61.

8. Gaston Bachelard, *The Poetics of Reverie*, trans. Daniel Russell (Beacon Press, 1960), 5.

9. Bachelard, *The Poetics of Reverie*, 75.

10. Louise Rosenblatt, *The Reader, The Text, The Poem* (Southern Illinois University Press, 1978), 21.

11. Bachelard, *The Poetics of Reverie*, 75 and 15.

12. Marion Milner, *A Life of One's Own* (Virago, 1934; 1986), 108–09.

13. Marshall Gregory, *Teaching Excellence in Higher Education* (Palgrave Macmillan, 2013), Chapter 6. I am quoting from the unpublished manuscript.

14. Charles Dickens, *Dombey and Son*, Ch. 11.

15. Image scanned by Philip V. Allingham for The Victorian Web. www.victorianweb.org/art/illustration/furniss/247.html.

16. William James, *The Varieties of Religious Experience* (Penguin, 1982), 499.

17. Roland Barthes, *The Pleasure of the Text*, trans. Richard Miller (Hill & Wang, 1975), 51.

18. Anne Carson, *Eros the Bittersweet* (Dalkey Archive Press, 1998), 50.

19. Galen Strawson, for example, might characterize someone like Steerforth as "Episodic." David's sense of his life as a story, with a consistent self moving through time, would be an example of a "Diachronic" personality. See Strawson, "Against Narrativity," *Ratio* 17.4 (Dec. 2004), pp. 428–52.

20. Frank Farrell, *Why Does Literature Matter?* (Cornell University Press, 2004), 17.

21. Marion Milner, 161.

22. Virginia Woolf, "David Copperfield," 77.

23. Iris Murdoch, "The Idea of Perfection," *Existentialists and Mystics*, ed. Peter Conradi (Penguin, 1998), 299.

24. Murdoch, 312–15. Italics in original.

25. John Forster, *The Life of Charles Dickens*, Vol. I, Ch. XX.

26. D. W. Winnicott, *Home is Where We Start From* (W. W. Norton, 1986), 47.

27. See Winnicott, 80–89.

28. Charles Dickens, *Selected Letters*, ed. Jenny Hartley (Oxford University Press, 2012), 283.

29. Winnicott, 46.

30. Jane Tompkins, *Reading Through the Night* (University of Virginia Press, 2018), 172.

31. Carson, 109.
32. Ibid.
33. Ibid., 106–7.
34. William James, "Is Life Worth Living," *Pragmatism and Other Essays* (Penguin, 2000), 238.
35. John Gardner, *On Moral Fiction* (Basic Books, 1978; 2000), 83–84.
36. Dickens, *Selected Letters*, 219.

Chapter 3

1. www.apa.org/news/press/releases/2020/10/election-stress.
2. www.vox.com/2021/1/28/22249273/trump-presidency-trauma-covid-19-2020-election.
3. D. W. Winnicott, *Home is Where We Start From: Essays by a Psychoanalyst* (W. W. Norton, 1986), 169.
4. Marion Milner, *An Experiment in Leisure* (Routledge, 2011), 169.
5. Winnicott, 175, 237.
6. Charles Dickens, *Little Dorrit* (Penguin, 2003), 416. For the convenience of readers using other editions, subsequent citations will be indicated parenthetically by book and chapter number.
7. Lionel Trilling, "*Little Dorrit*," *The Dickens Critics*, ed. George Ford and Lauriat Lane (Cornell University Press, 1961), 285.
8. James Hollis, *The Middle Passage: From Misery to Meaning* (Inner City Books, 1993), 116–17.
9. D. W. Winnicott, "Communicating and Not Communicating Leading to a Study of Certain Opposites," *The Maturational Processes and the Facilitating Environment: Studies in the Theory of Emotional Development* (Hogarth Press, 1965), 186. Original italics.
10. Rosemarie Bodenheimer, *Knowing Dickens* (Cornell University Press, 2007), 197, 200.
11. John Forster, *The Life of Charles Dickens*, Vol. II, Ch. XIX.
12. Gaston Bachelard, *The Poetics of Reverie: Childhood, Language and the Cosmos* (Beacon Press, 1971), 29.
13. Forster, Vol. I, Ch. 2.
14. John Carey, *The Violent Effigy: A Study of Dickens' Imagination* (Faber and Faber, 1973), 149.
15. Forster, Vol. I, Ch. 2.
16. Winnicott, "Communicating and Not Communicating," 187.

17. Ibid., 185.
18. Louise Bourgeois, *Destruction of the Father, Reconstruction of the Father: Writings and Interviews, 1923–1997*, eds. Marie-Laure Bernadac and Hans-Ulrich Obrist (The MIT Press1998), 133. Italics in original.
19. Christopher Bollas, *Cracking Up: The Work of Unconscious Experience* (Routledge, 1995), 87–88.
20. *The Selected Letters of Charles Dickens*, ed. Jenny Hartley (Oxford University Press, 2012), 283.
21. *Selected Letters of Charles Dickens*, 286.
22. Trilling, 289.
23. Rainer Maria Rilke, *Letters to a Young Poet*, trans. Stephen Mitchell (Random House, 1984), 78.
24. I can't trace the source for this quote, but I do say it all the time, and I thought it was Dorothy Parker.
25. Letter from Emily Dickinson to Thomas Wentworth Higginson, June 7, 1862. http://archive.emilydickinson.org/correspondence/higginson/l265.html.
26. www.culture24.org.uk/art/art379716; www.theartsdesk.com/visual-arts/louise-bourgeois-return-repressed-freud-museum; poesiegrenadine.com/poesiegrenadine/tag/Louise+Bourgeois; www.chloenelkin.wordpress.com/2012/03/17/bourgeois-through-freud-a-trip-to-maresfield-gardens/.
27. Michael Steig, *Dickens and Phiz* (Indiana University Press1978), 161.
28. Alice Miller, *The Drama of the Gifted Child: The Search for the Self*, trans. Ruth Ward (Basic Books, 1981), 22.
29. Milner, *An Experiment in Leisure*, 149, 150.
30. Sarton, *Journal of a Solitude* (W. W. Norton, 1973), 195.
31. Elizabeth Gaskell, *Mary Barton* (Oxford University Press, 2006), 62.
32. See "The Noble Savage" (*Household Words*, 1853) and "The Perils of Certain English Prisoners" (*Household Words*, 1857) as instances of Dickens's racist attitudes, as well as his letters about the 1857 Indian Rebellion.
33. "Anti-racism Statement of the Charles Dickens Society," January 8, 2021. https://dickenssociety.org/page/3.
34. Iris Murdoch, "The Idea of Perfection," *Existentialists and Mystics* (Penguin, 1997), 316–17.
35. Richard Rorty, "Heidegger, Kundera, Dickens," *Essays on Heidegger and Others* (Cambridge University Press, 1991), 81.

Chapter 4

1. Charles Dickens, *A Tale of Two Cities* (Penguin, 2003), p. 32. For the convenience of readers using other editions, subsequent citations will be indicated parenthetically by book and chapter number.
2. Charles Dickens, "A Christmas Carol," *Christmas Books* (Oxford World's Classics, 1988), 39.
3. Richard Rorty, "Heidegger, Kundera, and Dickens," *Essays on Heidegger and Others* (Cambridge University Press, 1991), 78.
4. From "The Tower," by William Butler Yeats.
5. Charles Dickens, *The Selected Letters of Charles Dickens*, ed. Jenny Hartley (Oxford University Press, 2012), 351.
6. Carol Gilligan, *The Birth of Pleasure: A New Map of Love* (Vintage Books, 2002), 28.
7. Jane Tompkins, *Reading Through the Night* (University of Virginia Press, 2018), 63.
8. Tompkins, 63.
9. William James, *The Varieties of Religious Experience* (Penguin, 1982), 169.
10. In *Past and Present* (1843), Thomas Carlyle wrote that the Hell of the English was "not making money." Dickens dedicated *Hard Times* to Carlyle.
11. Dickens, "A Christmas Carol," 38.
12. Gilligan, 31–32.
13. William James, "On a Certain Blindess in Human Beings," *Pragmatism and Other Essays* (Penguin, 2000), 273.
14. Peter Brooks, *The Melodramatic Imagination* (Yale University Press, 1995), 205.
15. John 15:13.

WORKS CITED

Bachelard, Gaston. *The Poetics of Space*. Trans. Maria Jolas. Penguin, 2014.

Bachelard, Gaston. *The Poetics of Reverie. Childhood, Language and the Cosmos*. Trans. Daniel Russell. Beacon Press, 1960.

Bart, Lionel (Lyrics). *Oliver!* Dir. Carol Reed. 1968. Shepperton Studios, UK. Amazon PrimeVideo.

Barthes, Roland. *The Pleasure of the Text*. Trans. Richard Miller. Hill & Wang, 1975.

Bayley, John. "*Oliver Twist*: 'Things as They Really Are.'" *Dickens and the Twentieth Century*. Eds. John Gross and Gabriel Pearson. Routledge, 1962. 49–64.

Bodenheimer, Rosemarie. *Knowing Dickens*. Cornell University Press, 2007.

Bollas, Christopher. *Cracking Up: The Work of Unconscious Experience*. Routledge, 1995.

Bourgeois, Louise. *Destruction of the Father, Reconstruction of the Father: Writings and Interviews, 1923–1997*. Eds. Marie-Laure Bernadac and Hans-Ulrich Obrist. The MIT Press, 1998.

Brooks, Peter. *The Melodramatic Imagination*. Yale University Press, 1995.

Carey, John. *The Violent Effigy: A Study of Dickens' Imagination*. Faber and Faber, 1973.

Carson, Anne. *Eros the Bittersweet*. Dalkey Archive Press, 1998.

Chandler, David. "Dickens on Wordsworth: *Nicholas Nickleby* and the Copyright Question." *English Language Notes* (2003) 41.1. 62–69.

Chekhov, Anton. *Fifty-Two Stories*. Trans. Richard Pevear and Larissa Volokhonsky. Vintage Classics, 2021.

Chotiner, Isaac. "Inside a Texas Building Where the Government Is Holding Immigrant Children," *The New Yorker*, June 22, 2019.

Dickens, Charles. *Oliver Twist*. Ed. Fred Kaplan. W. W. Norton, 1993.

Dickens, Charles. *A Tale of Two Cities*. Penguin, 2003.

Dickens, Charles. *David Copperfield*. Ed. Jerome H. Buckley. W. W. Norton, 1990.

Dickens, Charles. *Little Dorrit*. Penguin, 2003.

Dickens, Charles. *Christmas Books*. Oxford World's Classics, 1988.

Dickens, Charles. *The Selected Letters of Charles Dickens*. Ed. Jenny Hartley. Oxford University Press, 2012.

Farrell, Frank. *Why Does Literature Matter?* Cornell University Press, 2004.

Forster, John. *The Life of Charles Dickens*, Vols. I–III. Project Gutenberg.

Gardner, John. *On Moral Fiction*. Basic Books, 2000.

Gaskell, Elizabeth. *Mary Barton*. Oxford University Press, 2006.

Gilligan, Carol. *The Birth of Pleasure: A New Map of Love*. Vintage Books, 2002.

Gregory, Marshall. *Teaching Excellence in Higher Education*. Palgrave Macmillan, 2013.

Greene, Graham. *The Lost Childhood and Other Essays*. Viking, 1951.

Hollis, James. *The Middle Passage: From Misery to Meaning*. Inner City Books, 1993.

Hornback, Bert. "Frustration and Resolution in *David Copperfield*." *Studies in English Literature, 1500–1900*. 8.4 (Autumn 1968): 661–67.

Iser, Wolfgang. "The Reading Process: A Phenomenological Approach." *New Literary History* 3.2 (1972): 279–99.

James, Henry. *A Small Boy and Others*. Gibson Square Books, 2001.

James, William. *The Varieties of Religious Experience*. Penguin, 1982.

James, William. *Pragmatism and Other Essays*. Penguin, 2000.

Laux, Dorianne. *What We Carry*. Boa Editions, 1994.

Marcus, Steven. *Dickens from Pickwick to Dombey*. W. W. Norton, 1963.

Miller, Alice. *The Drama of the Gifted Child: The Search for the Self*. Trans. Ruth Ward. Basic Books, 1981.

Milner, Marion. *A Life of One's Own*. Virago, 1986.

Milner, Marion. *An Experiment in Leisure*. Routledge, 2011.

Mueller, Lisel. *Alive Together: New and Selected Poems*. Louisiana State University Press, 1996.

Murdoch, Iris. *Existentialists and Mystics*. Ed. Peter Conradi. Penguin, 1998.

Napolitano, Marc. *Oliver! A Dickensian Musical*. Oxford University Press, 2014.

Orwell, George. *A Collection of Essays*. Harvest, 1980.

Reed, Carol (Director). *Oliver!* 1968. Shepperton Studios, UK. Amazon Prime Video.

Rilke, Rainer Maria. *Letters to a Young Poet*. Trans. Stephen Mitchell. Random House, 1984.

Rorty, Richard. *Essays on Heidegger and Others*. Cambridge University Press, 1991.

Sarton, May. *Journal of a Solitude*. W. W. Norton, 1973.

Smith, Ali. *Artful*. Penguin, 2014.

Steig, Michael. *Dickens and Phiz*. Indiana University Press, 1978.

Tompkins, Jane. *Reading Through the Night*. University of Virginia Press, 2018.

Trilling, Lionel. "*Little Dorrit*." *The Dickens Critics*. Eds. George H. Ford and Lauriat Lane. Cornell University Press, 1961, 279–93.

Wilder, Thornton. *Our Town*. Harper Perennial, 2003.

Wills, Garry. "Love in the Lower Depths." *The New York Review of Books* (October 26, 1989).

Winnicott, D. W. *Home Is Where We Start From. Essays by a Psychoanalyst*. W. W. Norton, 1986.

Winnicott, D. W. "Communicating and Not Communicating Leading to a Study of Certain Opposites." *The Maturational Processes and the Facilitating Environment: Studies in the Theory of Emotional Development*. Hogarth Press, 1965.

Woolf, Virginia. *The Moment and Other Essays*. Harcourt Brace, 1947.

Woolf, Virginia. *The Second Common Reader*. Ed. Andrew McNeillie. Harcourt Brace Jovanovich, 1986.

ACKNOWLEDGMENTS

I gratefully acknowledge permission to reproduce the following:

Dorianne Laux, "For the Sake of Strangers" from *What We Carry*. Copyright © 1994 by Dorianne Laux. Reprinted by permission of The Permissions Company, LLC on behalf of BOA Editions, Ltd., boaeditions.org.

Lisel Mueller, "Missing the Dead" from *New and Selected Poems*. Copyright © 1996 by Lisel Mueller. Reprinted by permission of Louisiana State University Press.

"Be Back Soon." From the Musical Production–Rolumus Film *Oliver!* Words and Music by Lionel Bart © Copyright 1960 (Renewed); 1968 (Renewed). Lakeview Music Co. Ltd., London, England. TRO-Hollis Music, Inc. controls all publication rights for the U.S.A. and Canada. International Copyright Secured Made In U.S.A. All Rights Reserved Including Public Performance For Profit. Used by permission.

Louise Bourgeois, *The Dangerous Obsession* © 2021 The Easton Foundation / Licensed by VAGA at Artists Rights Society (ARS), NY.

Photograph of Little Dorrit's window in the Church of Saint George the Martyr, Southwark, London © Richard Jones, Discovery Tours and Events Ltd. www.london-walking-tours.co.uk. Thanks also to Canon Jonathan Sedgwick, Rector, Saint George the Martyr.

An Edna T. Shaeffer Award from the College of Arts and Letters at James Madison University helped fund this project. Thanks also to my kind and reassuring colleagues in the Department of English.

I would not have had the opportunity to write this book without the kindness and support of Jane Tompkins. She continues to inspire me. Thanks to the series editors of *My Reading* and to the great people at Oxford University Press. My deepest thanks to Philip Davis for his encouragement and trust.

Many cherished people in my life somehow found their way into this book about Charles Dickens. Those who have died continue to bless. Those still making the journey gladden the path, for myself and for others. I am so grateful for all of them.

INDEX